Clara's Grand

GLYNIS RIDLEY was born in Newcastle-upon-Tyne, studied in Edinburgh and Oxford, and has worked for the Open University, the University of Huddersfield, and Queen's University, Belfast. She now teaches eighteenth-century studies in the departments of English and Humanities at the University of Louisville, Kentucky. *Clara's Grand Tour* is her first book and was shortlisted for the Longman-History Today Award and the Duff Cooper Prize and is the winner of the Institute of Historical Research Prize.

FROM THE REVIEWS:

'A jewel of a story.' *New Scientist*

'Wonderful.' *Condé Nast Traveller*

'A remarkable book about a remarkable rhinoceros.' *Yorkshire Post*

'Charming.' *Scotland on Sunday*

'An exceptionally intelligent book ... Meticulous and unexpectedly moving.' *Washington Post*

'*Clara's Grand Tour* provides readers with an opportunity most often served up by the more thoughtful strains of historical fiction: namely, the chance to spend time in another, centuries-old reality and to emerge humbled, charmed and aware again of how very odd a place the world really is ... Glynis Ridley's book is a lovingly constructed portrait of an age when something as natural as a rhinoceros could enthrall all of Europe, from the illiterate and destitute to Frederick the Great and the vast, corrupt, sycophantic court at Versailles. The book's unspoken lesson is that with a little imagination, we can still find things - objects, people, animals, everyday phenomena - that might enthrall us just as deeply. Thanks, Clara, and thanks, Ridley. We needed that.' *San Francisco Chronicle*

'Reading this book, I rapidly became as fond of Clara as her owner no doubt was ... A worthy tribute to a remarkable creature who should not be forgotten.' Edwina Currie, *New Statesman*

Clara's Grand Tour

Travels with a Rhinoceros
in Eighteenth-Century Europe

GLYNIS RIDLEY

Atlantic Books
London

First published in Great Britain in 2004 by Atlantic Books,
an imprint of Grove Atlantic Ltd

This paperback edition published in 2005.

Copyright © Glynis Ridley 2004

The moral right of Glynis Ridley to be identified as
the author of this work has been asserted in accordance with
the Copyright, Designs and Patents Act of 1988.

Every effort has been made to trace or contact all copyright-holders.
The publishers will be pleased to make good any omissions or rectify any mistakes
brought to their attention at the earliest opportunity.

ISBN 1 84354 147 5

Printed and bound in Great Britain by Bookmarque Ltd, Croydon

Atlantic Books
An imprint of Grove Atlantic Ltd
Ormond House
26–27 Boswell Street
London WC1N 3JZ

Contents

Illustrations

Acknowledgements

An earlier version of this book was the recipient of the Institute for Historical Research (University of London) Prize. I would like to record sincere thanks to Toby Mundy and Angus MacKinnon of Atlantic Books, who both thought Clara's story worth telling and whose engagement with this project has been exemplary. Thanks also to Professor David Cannadine, Director of the Institute and Chair of the original judging panel, and to Samantha Jordan, who handled the emails, faxes and calls.

My understanding of the difficulties encountered by an eighteenth-century Dutch sea captain as he toured Europe with a rhinoceros was greatly increased by the experience of getting close to a pair of Indian rhinoceroses at Cincinnati Zoo. Thanks go to their keeper, Randy, who made this possible, and to Jimmy and Chenoweth, who provided, respectively, close-up front and rear views of their extraordinary hides. Jimmy was especially partial to having his nose scratched, and his curiosity and patience allowed me an unforgettable experience. Since the time of my visit to Cincinnati Zoo, the wonder of the eighteenth-century viewing public at seeing a rhinoceros seems very natural.

Many individuals have responded generously to my queries about their own areas of expertise or the historic collections in their care. Thanks are due to Delinda Buie of Library Special Collections, University of Louisville, Kentucky; Helen Chatterjee, University College London; Professor Kathleen Coleman of Harvard University; Dee Cook of the Society of Apothecaries, London; Yvonne Locke and Hannah Browne of the Barber Institute, University of Birmingham; Richard Redding of Redding Antiques, Zurich.

Friends have shared my enthusiasm for Clara's story. For inspiration, patience and asking pertinent questions which have helped determine some of the detail that follows, I would like to thank Ginny Hartery-Barker, Steve and Jayne Bostock, Lesley Jeffries, and Andrew Lewer. Monica Orr found in Rosewood the perfect place in which the writing could be completed. Jan Rizzuti took time out from her first European vacation to quiz an unsuspecting curator about the rhinoceros skeleton in his care. Mary Marcy truly went the extra mile.

At various times in researching *Clara's Grand Tour*, I needed help in translating source material. Two eighteenth-century scholars gave patiently of their time and knowledge. Andreas Müller took in his stride requests for translations of eighteenth-century German texts. John Patrick Greene undertook translations from French. In addition to being my French translator, John has shared the transatlantic commute, the zoo and museum visits, and negotiated with a number of *bouquinistes* to buy me my first original engraving of Clara. This book is dedicated to him.

Glynis Ridley
Belfast and Louisville, Kentucky, 2003

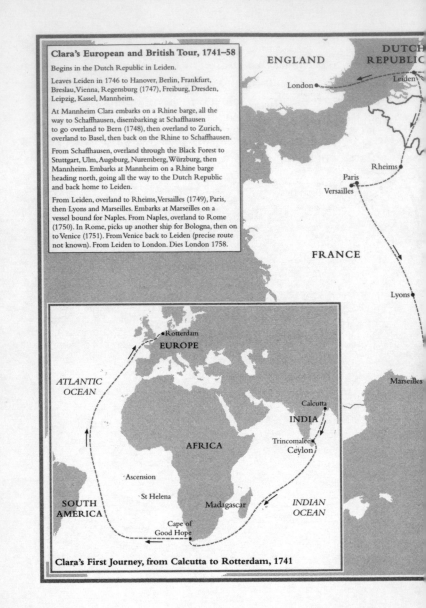

Clara's European and British Tour, 1741–58

Begins in the Dutch Republic in Leiden.

Leaves Leiden in 1746 to Hanover, Berlin, Frankfurt, Breslau, Vienna, Regensburg (1747), Freiburg, Dresden, Leipzig, Kassel, Mannheim.

At Mannheim Clara embarks on a Rhine barge, all the way to Schaffhausen, disembarking at Schaffhausen to go overland to Bern (1748), then overland to Zurich, overland to Basel, then back on the Rhine to Schaffhausen.

From Schaffhausen, overland through the Black Forest to Stuttgart, Ulm, Augsburg, Nuremberg, Würzburg, then Mannheim. Embarks at Mannheim on a Rhine barge heading north, going all the way to the Dutch Republic and back home to Leiden.

From Leiden, overland to Rheims, Versailles (1749), Paris, then Lyons and Marseilles. Embarks at Marseilles on a vessel bound for Naples. From Naples, overland to Rome (1750). In Rome, picks up another ship for Bologna, then on to Venice (1751). From Venice back to Leiden (precise route not known). From Leiden to London. Dies London 1758.

ENGLAND

DUTCH REPUBLIC

London

Leiden

Rheims

Paris

Versailles

FRANCE

Lyons

Marseilles

ATLANTIC OCEAN

Rotterdam

EUROPE

SOUTH AMERICA

AFRICA

Ascension

St Helena

Madagascar

Cape of Good Hope

Calcutta

INDIA

Trincomalee

Ceylon

INDIAN OCEAN

Clara's First Journey, from Calcutta to Rotterdam, 1741

Introduction

Patting a fully grown rhinoceros on the warm, relatively soft skin between its mouth and the base of its horn is not very obviously a form of historical research. But since the subject of this book is Clara, a three-ton Indian rhinoceros that became an eighteenth-century European sensation, and settled centuries of doubt about the appearance – indeed, the very existence – of the species, it did not seem strange that, one warm September day, I should find myself in close proximity to a pair of Indian rhino at Cincinnati Zoo.

As the male rhinoceros, Jimmy, inquisitively sniffed my hand and allowed me to feel his head, the skin hard as pumice-stone between the eyes, his female companion, Chenoweth, took a small branch in her mouth and turned her massive back towards me, unwittingly providing me with a close-up view of the unique texture and disposition of the hide. The keeper assured me that it was nothing personal; a female Indian rhinoceros is one of the most temperamental of all rhinos – a tendency exaggerated roughly every forty-five days of her hormonal cycle.

That anyone would voluntarily choose to travel with such an animal the length and breadth of Europe, as Clara's owner did, struck the keeper as a hard way to make a living. He had seen an African white rhino walk on cue at a park and, unlike the rest of the audience, he had been aware that this was perhaps the best that could be expected from any species of rhinoceros, since they are not the most co-operative or teachable of large animals. As Jimmy allowed two complete strangers to feel all around his massive head, and even seemed to enjoy the experience, Chenoweth kept a wary distance, working her way through the leafiest of lunches. Had I to choose one of the pair to work with, it would certainly not have been Chenoweth.

In the middle of the eighteenth century, an enterprising Dutch sea captain had succeeded where no one had before him and learned to work with Clara, a female Indian rhinoceros. Not only that, but he had also kept the animal healthy for almost two decades, during which time her display in front of everyone from the grandest of royals to the lowliest of peasants changed for ever the way that people imagined the rhinoceros. For, just as the British aristocracy undertook what was known as the Grand Tour – an extended period of travel to visit the most famous cultural sites of Europe deemed essential to round off an individual's education – so Clara undertook her own Tour, albeit as spectacle rather than as spectator, and she was duly immortalized in everything from high art to cheap wood-cuts, from the finest porcelain to tin coins.

Clara's Tour was brilliantly staged – and stage-managed. In fact, it presents a strong claim as one of the first recognizably modern media campaigns, with the rhino becoming the unwitting subject of a range of promotional literature and goods and, as her popularity periodically threatened to decline, of what were essentially advertising campaigns: releasing news of Clara's certain or imminent death, her owner would see a massive upsurge in interest, sympathy and, of course, bookings.

But just how on earth could a growing rhinoceros best be transported by land, sea or river in the eighteenth century? How could her co-operation be assured in front of the courts of Europe? What did Clara mean to those who saw her – did she represent a world of marvels quite beyond their own, or a challenge to their most fundamental theological and philosophical beliefs? And what does the eighteenth century's response to Clara tell us about our own attachment to the endangered natural world?

I had, of course, read about the travels and fame of Clara, but as I stood face to face with a similar animal, dwarfed by its height and its bulk, the fact that someone should spend seventeen years on the road displaying a rhinoceros in royal palaces and country inns, in places as far apart as London, Venice and Versailles, now seemed even more extraordinary than it had at first appeared.

CHAPTER I

First, Catch Your Rhino –
and Send It to Sea

The long sea journey from Calcutta to the Netherlands was finally over. On 22 July 1741, the Dutch sea captain Douwemout Van der Meer brought his ship the *Knabenhoe* into Rotterdam harbour and with it a most precious cargo, a young female Indian rhinoceros. From Van der Meer's decidedly entrepreneurial point of view, Clara's peculiar background was a cause for significant optimism. Only months old when her mother was killed by hunters somewhere in Assam in north-east India, Clara had been raised in the household of a director of the Dutch East India Company, J. A. Sichterman. As a party piece, Sichterman had allowed her to be taught to walk indoors, navigating her way round the elegant furniture, and to eat from a dinner plate. Yet there was obviously a limit to how

I

long this could continue to astonish and delight Sichterman's guests. To bring a rhino calf in with the cigars is one thing – to expect an adult rhino to negotiate an eighteenth-century dining room is quite another. Even as his guests applauded the novelty of a tame rhinoceros calf at dinner, Sichterman must have been aware that Clara, through no fault of her own, would soon become a liability indoors. What could be done with her?

Accustomed to taking food from humans since she was weaned, Clara would perhaps have stood little chance if returned to the plains of Assam, though in understanding Sichterman's decision to sell her to a visiting Dutch sea captain, a word of caution is probably in order. We live in a world in which species are endangered and in which breeding and re-introduction programmes seek to restore chosen animals to their native habitats. Sicheterman and Van der Meer represent an eighteenth-century mindset that had no conception of the natural world as finite. Even rhinoceroses were abundantly available here – though stubbornly resistant to their own exploitation. Enterprising citizens of a great trading nation, the company director and sea captain could no more have contemplated releasing a young rhino back into the wild than they could have thought of her humane destruction. Once used to humans, a young, healthy rhinoceros represented a rare commercial opportunity. Believing that a rhinoceros could live for at least a hundred years, and knowing that Clara was no more than three, Van der Meer must have dreamed of a lifetime's income. Surely everyone would wish to see a rhinoceros? Van der Meer had simply to find an effective means of transporting and advertising his investment.

From the third to the sixteenth centuries AD, no rhinoceros was seen on European soil and the skills of the Roman animal handlers who had previously brought the animal to Europe were lost. Scholars expressed doubts about the existence of the elusive creature, which was said by classical writers to be the arch-enemy of the elephant, and thought to possess a horn of incredible medicinal power. The only way to resolve uncertainties about the existence and nature of the rhinoceros was to capture one alive and bring it to Europe. But the difficulties of capturing a rhinoceros in the wild paled into insignificance compared to the problems posed by transporting such a large animal by sea or horse-drawn wagon. Once caught, an animal had to be kept in good health and secured on board a pitching sailing ship for the six-month voyage from India to Europe. Assuming that a ship finally made landfall in Europe with its live cargo intact, an overland journey would then be required. In an era wholly dependent upon sail and horse power, the logistics of moving a rhinoceros were daunting. Elephants had been bred in captivity in Europe since Roman times, but the rhinoceros was the rarest of live imports. Small wonder, then, that from the Renaissance until the end of the eighteenth century, only eight rhinoceroses survived the journeys from their native homes long enough to be displayed to curious European audiences.

Those eight rhinoceroses had one thing in common: all were Indian rhino. The specific characteristics of the Indian rhino will gradually emerge in the course of Clara's story, but there were good reasons for why these animals were obtained from India and not Africa. Five species of rhinoceros survive in the world today: the Sumatran and Javan rhino are both reclusive forest dwellers and so rare that few of us will ever see them in the flesh. The Sumatran rhino is covered in coarse, reddish hair and is the most ancient of all surviving rhino species. Sixteenth-century European explorers almost certainly did not know of the existence of either of these. Africa is home to two species of rhino – the black and the white rhino – and today both are found only in sub-Saharan Africa. Both have two horns at the end of their nose, in contrast to the single horn of the Indian rhinoceros. It is known that the Romans sourced a species of white rhino from Africa *north* of the Sahara – a population confined there by the encroachments of the desert across millennia – but the inexhaustible appetite of the Roman games seems to have been responsible for wiping out these herds.

As European statesmen, scholars and artists experienced a widespread renaissance of interest in the classical Graeco-Roman world (an interest variously held to have started in the fifteenth or sixteenth centuries), they must have wondered about the truth of ancient texts that described a near-invincible horned animal, as large as the elephant. It should have been possible to acquire rhinoceroses from sub-Saharan Africa, but prior to the nineteenth century, the European powers sought to exploit Africa primarily for slaves and safe harbours. Any African animals brought from the interior were more often than not single specimens, conspicuously lacking in the sort of bulk and ferocity that made transportation overland both time-consuming and complex. African tribes such as the Masai had long ago honed the combination of skills necessary to approach a wild rhino, to prove hunting prowess, but no European expedition had made contact with any tribe that was both willing and able to undertake the capture of a rhino, unharmed, and to shepherd it across country for the benefit of white traders. Not until the British began laying railway lines across their African colonies in the nineteenth century would the modern exploitation of Africa's big game begin.

When Renaissance men read Roman writers' descriptions of the rhinoceros, last seen in Europe in the second century, there was therefore only one place that could be envisaged as a source of supply: India. Happily for Europe's power-brokers, trade networks within India, and between India and Europe's sea-faring powers, were well established, even in the sixteenth century. That the single-horned Indian rhinoceros is the largest of the five species

GLYNIS RIDLEY

of rhinoceros and perhaps the most difficult to work with is something of which early modern Europeans were certainly unaware. Having no choice in the matter, but wishing desperately to bring a live rhinoceros to Europe, statesmen and traders therefore determined to obtain an Indian animal and to grow rich through its display.

The present-day international boundaries of India may be a twentieth-century creation, but its great provinces still provide an indication of the key princedoms with which pre-industrial Europe sought to trade: the Delhi Sultanate, Gujarat, Bengal. Prior to the rise of the Mughal Empire (which was taken over by the British), regional antagonisms within the sub-continent had pitted the princes of Delhi against invading Tartar forces and there is evidence that rhinoceroses (and elephants) were deployed in battle by the Delhi Sultanate as early as the fourteenth century. With tridents attached to their heads, such animals seem to have had a largely symbolic function: the prince who could command a phalanx of rhino signalled his power as effectively as a modern superpower capable of deploying the latest battle hardware.

But how could a rhinoceros be controlled in battle, even if control meant simply avoiding wreaking havoc amongst its own ranks? An illustration of an Indian rhino seen in London in 1684 is anatomically inaccurate, for the rhino has been given a pair of outsized human ears and a very human nose and mouth, suggesting that the artist was working

6

from a second-hand report. But the animal is wearing the paraphernalia of leg irons and has a ring through its nose, which suggests that, just like a bull, a rhinoceros might be rendered more co-operative by the insertion of such a ring while it is still a largely defenceless calf. As it is, 70 per cent of the vast head of a rhinoceros is dedicated to its olfactory organs, the sense of smell being the most acute of this animal's senses. Indeed, to touch the head of a rhino is to be made instantly aware of the importance and sensitivity of the nose, which eagerly seeks out the smell of something, or someone, new. Here the skin is at its thinnest and, whilst it is not soft by any means, the contrast between its relative mobility and the rock-hard texture of the upper head and everything behind it is striking. (In contrast to the Indian rhino, both species of African rhino have a uniformly smooth skin that lacks the protective qualities of the Indian rhino's almost continuous three-inch hide.)

When European traders began trying to obtain rhinoceroses from India, the princes with whom they bargained had at their command animal trainers every bit as expert as the Roman handlers who managed wild animals for the Roman Games. Yet whilst it was in theory possible to buy a rhinoceros in India, the transportation of such an animal to Europe presented formidable problems. Uniquely among the eight animals that survived the journey from the sixteenth to the eighteenth centuries, Clara was caught and transported whilst still a calf. All of the other seven animals appear to have reached their mature height and weight prior to their sea voyages, presenting their captors with an immediate three-ton headache. Just where and how can a rhinoceros best be stowed on a sailing ship?

Ocean-going sailing ships might appear to have had vast expanses of empty deck and capacious holds. The reality was rather different. The deck was crammed with animal pens to provide the crew with food, and the hold was filled with cargo to ensure the economic viability of the journey. Seamen were typically allotted a space eighteen inches wide for hammocks that they occupied on a strictly regulated shift system. Sailing from India to Europe before the cutting of the Suez Canal, a ship had to endure the sweltering heat of the tropics and then round the Cape of Good Hope to sail the length of Africa a second time. From the west African coast, the prevailing currents sweep out into the Atlantic: it is not easy to hug the coast, heading for Europe, and still less easy if your cargo is alive and temperamental, acting as unpredictable moving ballast. Slaving ships were designed to forestall such problems by stacking tightly fettered slaves on wooden slats which had a vertical clearance of only two and a half feet, thus removing any possibility of movement. In transporting sought-after Arabian horses from east to west, European traders had arrived at a formula of allowing a prize horse some eight times more room than that given to a slave, and had learned how to winch the highly strung animals on board and secure them with minimal risk of damage.

Just as Arabian horses were considered less expendable than slaves, so a rhinoceros was infinitely more valuable than even the princely gift of a thoroughbred. It might seem reasonable to assume that rare animals were stowed in the hold, away from the extremes of temperature and driving spray experienced intermittently on deck, but the available evidence contradicts this. Dry cargoes such as tea or cloth were packed into a hold from which light and air were excluded. On slaving ships, the live cargo was similarly deprived of light and air since slavers were only concerned with the fate of the bulk of those being transported: the death of an individual slave was of no great import. But prize animals, considered infinitely more precious than slaves, needed both fresh air and light, and the only place to guarantee this was on deck, in pens and cages next to the regular livestock.

That successive rhinoceroses were caged on the decks of sailing ships appears to be confirmed by reports of the journey of an animal intended for the royal menagerie at Versailles in the late eighteenth century: the 1769–70 log of the *Duc de Praslin* notes that the rhinoceros had become tolerant of the presence of a goat which it would allow to eat hay from between its legs. The anecdote says much about the conditions in which rhinoceroses bound for Europe were transported. Since domestic livestock such as chickens and goats were allowed some freedom of movement on deck to prevent them running to fat, the fact that a goat could wander in and out from between a rhinoceros's legs suggests that the rhino was secured on deck in a cage with wide bars – iron being an obvious candidate for the cage's construction as a wooden crate could simply have been kicked to pieces. And as domestic animals were typically penned at the fore of a ship, we can place the eight rhinoceroses here too – a sight to which a ship's crew could have only accustomed itself with difficulty.

A rhinoceros will naturally seek out water or mud during the day to cool itself and moisturize its skin. But fresh water was far too precious a commodity on board a ship to be wasted in this way, and so an animal subjected to the baking heat of the tropics and spattered with the residue of salty spray would quickly dehydrate. Fish oil therefore became a mud substitute and was applied to the hide on a daily basis; the disadvantage of the smell had to be offset against the continued good health of the passenger. A canvas canopy would have been rigged over the cage to keep off the worst of the sun, and lowered to keep the animal calm during periods of intense activity on deck and in the rigging overhead. Yet it is one thing to cage a rhinoceros on the fore deck of a ship, quite another to secure its good behaviour. What sort of travelling companion is a rhinoceros?

Look for images of the rhinoceros in western culture and it will quickly become apparent that we are the unwitting heirs of misconceptions that can be traced back to Roman writers. Pliny claimed in his *Natural History* that the rhinoceros and the elephant were mortal enemies, and that a rhinoceros would not hesitate to gore an elephant, even completely unprovoked. He established a paradigm that continues to permeate literature, art and advertising in surprising ways. Successful children's stories see Babar the elephant pitted against his arch-enemy, Lord Rataxes of Rhinoland; whilst in Roald Dahl's *James and the Giant Peach* James has the early misfortune of being orphaned when his parents are eaten by a rhinoceros escaped from the zoo. Elephants are regarded as gentle, wise and dependable, rhinoceroses as powerful, brutal and stupid. When the surrealist playwright Eugene Ionesco wished to represent a community falling victim to the rise of fascism, he imagined a provincial French town whose inhabitants gradually metamorphose into unthinking rhinoceroses, intent on running with the herd. Throughout *Rhinocéros*, the animals are seen as destructive, grotesque and ultimately terrifying. Yet after the Palace of Versailles had fallen to the French Revolutionaries in 1789 and the natural historian Buffon found himself able to take a stroll around the royal menagerie, he reported that the rhinoceros that had been Louis XVI's pride and joy would eagerly come to the bars of its cage to be patted.

When not defending its territory or young, a mature rhinoceros is far from its cultural stereotype. Furthermore, Clara was not a fully grown adult when she first became accustomed to human society. And because a rhino calf is dependent upon its mother for perhaps the first two years of its life, anyone fulfilling the motherly role of providing food during this time will find in the calf a dedicated follower. This is a recognized form of total dependence by one species upon another that psychologists refer to as 'imprinting'.

Where Clara's fellow rhino transportees tested their captors' resourcefulness to its limits, Clara imprinted upon the people around her, quickly becoming accepting of human society. An iron cage secured to the fore deck of the *Knabenhoe* may have been her home on the voyage from India to Europe, but it provided her with a safe berth as the ship pitched violently in the waters of the Cape. In fact, as far as the safety of those around her was concerned, there was no need to keep this rhinoceros behind bars. Men were to Clara the complete mother substitute, in so far as they could ever fulfil this role: providers of food and attendant upon her every recognizable need. Clara accepted human society, so her distress was probably minimal compared to that experienced by her mature counterparts. Considering that none of the crew who sailed with her to Europe had ever seen a rhinoceros before, it must have seemed marvellous that this animal would tamely fix upon the nearest ration of beer (already an acquired taste, to be sniffed out under any circumstances) and tobacco (an apparently mesmerizing smell), standing by in the hope of a suitable reward. If the thought of habituating a wild animal to such potentially addictive pleasures strikes a modern audience as repellent, it should be remembered that while fresh water was so precious at sea, regular allowances of ale were seen as necessary liquid nourishment for the crew. Lacking any sense that the quantity of beer or tobacco they consumed might do them any harm, the sailors who doubtless laughed at Clara's dietary preferences cannot have seen anything wrong in giving her a taste of what they themselves enjoyed.

Besides, Clara was undoubtedly the most important passenger on board and the one whose needs had to be met at all costs. Never had such a rare animal been so co-operative with its captors and so tolerant of their presence. As he sailed his ship home, Douwemout Van der Meer could observe Clara daily and accustom her to take food from him. So began a relationship that would last for eighteen years, leading Van der Meer into the company of kings and fixing once and for all the European conception of the rhinoceros.

CHAPTER 2

Of Anatomists and Advertising –
At Home in Holland

'Behold now Behemoth, which I made with thee;
he eateth grass as an ox.'
Job 41: 15

As Van der Meer sailed home, the everyday care of
Clara on board the *Knabenhoe* would have struck him as
a relatively straightforward matter compared to the
difficulties he anticipated in Leiden. Though a mid-
eighteenth-century nobleman might have commanded
wealth and influence enough to keep a large, exotic animal
within the close confines of a city, at this stage of his life
Van der Meer was without either money or civic status.
Indeed, had his family been wealthy, the young sea captain
would no doubt have left more than the sparse records in the
archives of Leiden that suggest the outlines of his earlier

life. Born in 1705, Van der Meer must have joined the influential Dutch East India Company at an early age in order to have risen through the ranks as he had. After the fact of his birth, he next appears in official paperwork in 1741, when he left the Company at the age of thirty-six in order to devote his life to displaying Clara.

Van der Meer had done little or nothing, then, to attract the attention of the good citizens of Leiden – until he attempted to stable a rhinoceros in their midst. Across eighteenth-century Europe, city councils were beginning to consider the matter of civic hygiene with varying degrees of seriousness, and not all authorities would have been prepared to indulge an ordinary citizen in his wish to house a rhinoceros within a city's bounds. But Leiden was remarkable for its tolerant civic culture in two respects, both of which were to prove beneficial to a sea captain of humble beginnings who hoped to better his lot.

Leiden was one of the great centres of the European print trade: prominent city families such as the Luchtmans had, for generations, been printing and selling works written in French by some of the most controversial thinkers of successive ages. If their business was firmly rooted in the tolerant traditions of the city, however, their clientele was truly international. As Van der Meer brought Clara home, the Luchtmans' bookshops competed with perhaps as many as thirty others in Leiden: the city possessed a university of international repute and was hungry for the latest knowledge; it was also filled with businessmen eager to get that knowledge into print.

Furthermore, across the Dutch Republic, groups of merchants and gentlemen were banding together to form learned societies. To the amazement of foreign visitors, it seemed that membership of these societies, or attendance at one of their meetings, was not limited to men of a certain class: anyone with an interest in a given topic was welcome to attend. The scope of these societies' interests may be gauged by the fact that one – *Linguaque Animoque Fideles* – was formed in Leiden in 1759, dedicated to the advancement of the Dutch language, natural history and literature: subjects that had no chairs at the university but were thought important enough to warrant dedicated investigation. In bringing Clara to Leiden, Van der Meer brought the new and the strange to a city whose commerce and intellectual exchange depended upon the transmission of new discoveries and ideas. The civic delegates representing the sixty-four districts or 'quarters' of the city had only to let their curiosity get the better of them and see Clara in the flesh to be convinced that she posed no danger to their fellow citizens. Van der Meer would be allowed to stable her near the city's boundaries, where civic and private outbuildings gave way to flat pastureland. For Van der Meer – and Clara – the arrangement was ideal.

Since a rhinoceros is hardly an impulse buy, it is only reasonable to assume that Van der Meer had significant plans for his purchase. A male rhinoceros had been put on display in London in 1739 but it is impossible to look at the various representations made of it without detecting a misery to which its eighteenth-century keepers were blind. A poor specimen in every sense, it died in 1741, just as Clara began her own European odyssey. Indeed, this was the spectre that haunted Van der Meer's early years with Clara: since the fall of the Roman Empire, no one had managed to bring a rhinoceros to Europe *and* keep it alive long enough to understand anything about the care of the species.

Clara's first years in Leiden may seem devoid of any great incident, but it is worth remembering that for Van der Meer himself they would have been full of drama. Each morning he would have asked himself the same nagging question as he opened the stable door: would he find Clara still alive? And if Van der Meer were to succeed in discovering the means whereby she could be kept alive, when all others before him had failed, could he afford those means? Leiden's thriving print culture provides both a graphic demonstration of how Clara survived and an indication of how Van der Meer would finance her early upkeep.

Clara arrived in Leiden in 1741, but the earliest known images of her – crudely produced woodcuts and more sophisticated copper engravings that were undoubtedly commissioned by Van der Meer – date from the period 1746–9. It seems unlikely that Van der Meer would have waited five years from the date of Clara's safe arrival in

Europe to start promoting and displaying her. And if he was aiming at quality as well as quantity among his paying customers, were such woodcuts the best means of generating interest in the most profitable social quarters? Fortunately for Van der Meer, it transpires that he did not have to dig into his own pockets to produce the first high-quality advertisement for Clara. For in 1741–2, another native of Leiden saw the potential of using Clara's image to advertise his own line of business. The earliest known image of Clara is, then, not a grainy woodcut from 1746, but a very fine copper engraving, which also happens to be a page from an anatomy textbook.

The University of Leiden was widely known and respected throughout Europe. From 1593, it had boasted the first Dutch anatomy theatre, frequent engravings of which gave prominence to the Latin text *Nosce te Ipsum* ('Know Thyself') to provide a spiritual dimension to the pursuit of medical knowledge. The practices of Dutch medical schools had also been immortalized in oil more than once, but most famously in Rembrandt van Rijn's large 1632 canvas, *The Anatomy Lesson of Dr Tulp*. Here an Amsterdam anatomist dissects a human cadaver for the benefit of his students and interested (paying) members of the public alike. In the centre of a gaggle of onlookers, Rembrandt pictures Tulp in the process of opening a human body, attempting to understand its inner workings and demonstrate them to his audience.

But to treat anatomy first and foremost as merely a spectacle for the curious is to overlook its primary purpose as a teaching tool. For medical students down the centuries, the dissection of a human body has proved an invaluable means of learning what medical textbooks alone could not teach. And as anatomical understanding advanced, largely through repeated experiment and methodical investigation, so anatomical textbooks became more sophisticated, seeking ways to represent layers of muscle and tendon in sequence, all the way down to the bone.

The first modern anatomical atlas, and one of the very greatest, is widely held to be Andreas Vesalius's *De humani corporis fabrica* from 1543. Giving precise directions to his engraver, Calcar, the anatomist Vesalius oversaw the production of a series of illustrated plates in which a male body is progressively stripped of its musculature, eventually revealing the skeletal framework which anchors the whole. Were the flaying of the body represented as a static procedure, Vesalius's atlas would not have achieved quite the degree of fame it has. What makes it impossible to forget Vesalius's 'muscle man' is that he is posed against a landscape background. As layer upon layer of muscle is exposed, only to be stripped away in the next engraved plate, the body continues, improbably, to strike a series of poses, intended to highlight the key muscle groups concerned. An initial sense that we are watching a grotesque dance of death is replaced by fascination at the ingenuity of both the body and the engraver – this is, physically at least, the essence of what we are but not the sum total of who we are, as the 'life' of Vesalian man continues beyond the grave. Vesalius's *De humani corporis fabrica* was both a revelation and the blueprint for a new generation of anatomical texts.

With a flourishing university medical school, Leiden had need of good anatomists and the most modern textbooks, though medical students were by no means the only market for the latest works. What is today termed 'science' was then thought of as 'natural philosophy' and a literate man who took an interest in the world around him would have understood the questions posed by, say, anatomy and history to be of essentially the same nature. The thrust of such questions was inevitably intended to grope towards understanding of the greatest imponderable of all: the meaning of life.

To the eighteenth-century mind, a search for the meaning of life clearly involved understanding how life worked. So the injunction 'Know Thyself' associated with Leiden's anatomy theatre had a philosophical as well as a physical dimension, and the audience in one of Dr Tulp's anatomy theatres was therefore as likely to include the philosopher and the historian as it was the medical student. And if a self-made man of business who had not had the advantage of a private tutor and university education also wished to learn more about the world around him, the exploding print culture gave him a wealth of texts in his own language (as opposed to Latin and Greek), often with handsome illustrations of the latest 'scientific' understanding. A good-quality, eighteenth-century anatomical atlas had more than the fledgling medical community in its publisher's sights.

Just as Van der Meer was gambling on Europe-wide public interest in the display of a live rhinoceros, so the gifted and ambitious Dutch anatomist B. S. Albinus was hoping to produce the definitive anatomical atlas of the time. Across Europe, lazy and impecunious publishers were bringing out anatomical textbooks which fed market demand by the simple expedient of marrying old engravings with textual commentaries for which the engravings were not designed. If Vesalius had set a standard in 1543, it was one which was rarely matched in the two hundred years that followed. From the first, Albinus intended his work to be different to the shameless productions of lesser anatomists: an eighteenth-century Vesalius with a modern text complemented by high-quality illustrations. The degree of Albinus's commitment to his anatomical atlas may be gauged by the fact that he would spend 24,000 florins on its production but only 15,000 on his house in Leiden.

Both Van der Meer and Albinus doubtless gazed out across the prosperous Leiden cityscape of medieval timbered houses and modern, gabled red brick as they pondered their situation. Each man had an idea, a plan, he hoped would bring him wealth and fame, but each knew that he had to make a considerable financial investment before he could recoup any profit. If only, then, he could generate some income: if only Van der Meer could drum up interest in Clara whilst ensuring she continued in good health; and if only Albinus could generate interest in his forthcoming book whilst continuing to obtain suitable specimens and pay for first-rate engravings of them. Such mutual need would inspire a mutually satisfying solution.

This first picture of Clara is of strikingly good quality. It is not a crudely executed print giving little variation of light and shade. Rather, the image suggests both a depth of field and different textures within it, from the stone wall and the leafy branches to the smoothness of bone and leatheriness of hide. That such variation and accuracy can be achieved by the patient carving of a wooden block, or by an engraver's burin cutting into a copper plate, is perhaps nothing short of miraculous. (The eighteenth-century writer and artist William Blake would develop a different technique again, using acid to eat out the design in the copper.) Whichever technique the engraver employs, each cut represents an expensive and time-consuming commitment to the finished product. The writer draws a line through an unwanted word, crumples up an unwanted sheet, or nowadays hits the 'delete' key. The engraver cannot try the look of different alternatives, neither have the majority of engravers historically been able to afford to waste the raw materials of their art. The detail of a fine engraving is therefore likely to be significant – to mean something.

What, then, does this picture of Clara mean? And how do we know that it was drawn from life? The two questions are impossible to separate.

Rhinoceroses had appeared in art long before Clara arrived in Leiden. The only problem with the majority of these depictions is that, in the absence of a live – or even dead – model, artists had to rely on second-hand descriptions, from individuals who had seen a rhinoceros, or from literature in which the animals were described. The perils of illustrating something from someone else's description are best illustrated by one of the most famous pictures of a rhinoceros in Western art: Albrecht Dürer's woodcut of 1515. Over two hundred years after its production, this image was still being copied by artists who needed to depict a rhinoceros. Indeed, it is hardly an exaggeration to say that, wherever the image of a rhinoceros is encountered from the sixteenth to the early eighteenth centuries, it probably has its origin in Dürer's woodcut.

The infallible test of this is whether the animal has a horn rising from its back above the shoulders, as Dürer's specimen so clearly has. Dürer had never seen a rhinoceros himself and relied on the report of someone who claimed to have seen a rhinoceros landed at Lisbon in 1515. But the engraved plate from Albinus's anatomical atlas shows an animal without a dorsal horn or the exaggerated armour plating of Dürer's imagining. The rhinoceros on the plate does not, therefore, have Dürer as its origin. Even a cursory comparison of Dürer's woodcut with Jan Wandelaar's engraving will indicate that Wandelaar's animal is more realistic – more natural. Where Dürer engraves an archetype entitled simply 'rhinoceros', since it is emblematic of the species, Wandelaar engraves a particular animal. Clara, newly arrived in Leiden, is captured as she grazes her way through the day, eating to put on the weight of a healthy, growing rhinoceros. Wandelaar's engraving is unmistakably drawn from life and, as the only rhinoceros available for him to copy in Leiden in 1741 was Clara, this is undoubtedly her. But if we can agree that this is drawn from life, what does the image mean? Why did both Albinus and Van der Meer seek to have Clara represented in this way?

Wandelaar's engraving was one of only two to be put on sale separately from the anatomical atlas for which they were both finally intended: Albinus's *Tabulae sceleti et musculorum corporis humani* of 1747. Crucially, the image of Clara, along with that of the skeleton of a young human male, was in the shops of Leiden in 1742, one year after her arrival in the town and five years before Albinus's complete text would appear. Appearing singly in this way, Wandelaar's image could be seen as an accomplished precursor of a twentieth-century promotion. For the picture of Clara can be read as an advertisement for both the forthcoming atlas (in which it is easily the most intriguing and one of the most technically accomplished plates) and

Clara's projected tour. Even citizens of Leiden who would buy neither the single image nor, in the fullness of time, the whole of Albinus's atlas would be exposed to the print in the windows of the bustling city's printers and booksellers, and would have plenty of time to decide that they, too, must see Van der Meer's extraordinary creature.

On one level, then, the engraving acts as a flier or an advertisement for both Albinus's *Tabulae* and Van der Meer's display of Clara. But the image also works in a more subtle way to promote Van der Meer's interests. Like Hamlet mesmerized by Yorick's skull, we look at the foreground skeleton and realize, To this will it come – this is what will physically remain when flesh and blood are gone. And what is true for the viewer of the image is true for Clara also – underneath her three-inch-thick hide, she is flesh and blood and bone and is subject to the same processes of decay that the human skeleton represents. Had not the London rhinoceros only lasted two years on display? Foreshadowing Van der Meer's later media manipulations, the image reminds us that Clara may look indestructible, but she too is mortal – so pay your money while you can if you want to see a live rhinoceros.

Through Wandelaar's engraving, Van der Meer's rhino calf was introduced to an unsuspecting public. Like any media icon of our own television age, Clara would quickly prove her bankability by simultaneously generating and feeding a public appetite, the scale of which had simply not been anticipated. Given that both Van der Meer and Albinus were playing for high stakes with little capital, it is easy to imagine the two men's satisfaction when Wandelaar's engraving appeared around Leiden. Where Albinus could point to the copper engraving as the embodiment of all he hoped that his future textbook would be, Van der Meer could reflect on his ownership of that rarest of eighteenth-century commodities: a tame and apparently healthy rhinoceros. The marketing of Clara had begun.

To realize his dreams of making a lucrative income from her display, Van der Meer had only to overcome the two obstacles that had prevented anyone previously capitalizing on a live rhinoceros on European soil: Clara had to be kept alive and a means had to be found for transporting all three tons of her across thousands of miles of unforgiving, primitive coaching roads. As he wrestled with these practical matters, Van der Meer surely had no conception that the very fact of Clara's existence would pose problems of a different sort and would place both owner and rhinoceros at the centre of philosophical and theological disputes about the natural world. But all that lay in the future. For now, Clara had simply to be fed.

Wandelaar's engraving gives some insight into how Van der Meer succeeded in keeping a rhinoceros alive where all other Europeans since the fourth century had failed. To begin to describe the engraving is unwittingly to start listing a series of oppositions – man and beast, bone and hide, vertical and horizontal, foliage and wall, and so on. And out of these oppositions, what seems a cruel irony emerges: if Clara's living, breathing flesh is in bulky contrast to the skeleton's bone, she continues to feed that growing flesh even as the skeleton averts his eyeless gaze. A rhinoceros must eat to live, as must we all, but the naturalism of Clara's pose points us to another truism: a rhinoceros lives to eat.

The majority of herbivores are ruminants, possessing a multi-chambered stomach which has more than one chance to extract the rich variety of nutrients (and, inevitably, the toxins) contained in plant material. What cannot be broken down in one part of the gut may yet be digested in another. The rhinoceros is a herbivore but not a ruminant; indeed, it possesses a very primitive digestive system in comparison with other herbivores. The beneficial effects of any nutrients that resist being broken down in its single stomach are denied the rhinoceros for ever, but so are the adverse effects of any toxins. The great advantage of this to the animal is that it can comfortably eat a range of plant species that many ruminants find unpalatable. In the unforgiving Namibian desert, for example, pockets of African black rhino survive some of the harshest conditions on earth today by feasting on the fleshy grey-green leaves of the milk-bush plant (*Euphorbia tirucalli*). It is not the potentially threatening bulk of the black rhino that ensures it has the milk-bush to itself; rather, its grazing rights are assured by the fact that all other animals find the milk-bush acutely toxic. If the rhinoceros had a more 'advanced' digestive tract, it too would find the plant poisonous.

As a species, then, the rhinoceros presents its keepers with a feeding paradox: it can eat a wider variety of vegetation than most herbivores, but the digestive process that allows this licence does so because the rhinoceros is less efficient at extracting nutrients from what it eats than other plant eaters. To grow and thrive, a rhinoceros needs to eat far more than would a ruminant of similar size. And as one of the largest land mammals on the planet, the Indian rhino must eat prodigious quantities of vegetation in order to maintain itself in peak condition – at least 150 pounds a day. A young rhino, like Clara in 1742, must therefore feed constantly in order to grow. Removed from their natural habitats and the rich variety of plant material to which they were accustomed, those of Clara's predecessors that survived the journey to Europe almost certainly became progressively more under-nourished as their captivity continued. The male rhinoceros displayed in London from 1739 until its death in 1741 seems to have eaten enough whilst on display to give the impression that he was well fed: the reality is that his massive frame probably lacked sufficient quantities of a vital range of nutrients to sustain health, and ultimately life itself.

Given all this, it is tempting to feel morally and intellectually superior to those who, from the sixteenth to the eighteenth centuries, struggled unsuccessfully to keep a succession of prized rhinoceroses alive. Yet before condemning Van der Meer's predecessors for their ignorance – one which may have been responsible for the premature deaths of at least four animals – it is worth remembering that knowledge of an animal's physiology and genuine concern for its wellbeing do not in themselves guarantee a healthy, happy specimen. Some two and a half centuries later, it would take the deaths of half of the Sumatran rhino captured for a breeding programme started in 1984 (these twenty rhino comprised a fortieth of the known Sumatran rhino population) before those desperate to conserve the species finally understood that the captive rhino seemed to need a greater quantity of fresh fibre than they would ordinarily seek out in the wild. What initially appears to be one of the most robust herbivores on the planet is in fact one of the most acutely sensitive to the conditions of its captivity.

When he first encountered Clara at the wealthy Sichterman's home, Van der Meer no doubt took careful note of the quantity and quality of what she ate. What, he must have asked himself, might replace the lush, tropical vegetation of Assam, with its evergreen forests and dense swathes of grasses and bamboos? So it seems more than coincidental that the very first image of Clara should capture her grazing. The anatomist's skeletal model doubtless stood rigid in the engraver's studio, permanently available at the artist's convenience, his bones wired and his physical requirements non-existent. (And looking through all of the plates of Albinus's anatomical atlas, it becomes possible to recognize this overworked and undemanding model by his unvarying pose across a range of plates.) But Wandelaar's studio would have been no place for a live rhinoceros, even assuming a limitless supply of hay. It would never have been big enough. Instead, Van der Meer must have led the engraver to a stable and adjoining pasture where permission had been secured for Clara to graze. Accustomed as she was to people rather than other rhino, the artist and his sketch pad were far less interesting to Clara than the fresh grass that she could smell all around. So when Wandelaar moved his position to allow him to sketch both front and rear views of Van der Meer's extraordinary animal, Clara was not perturbed in the slightest.

Throughout Clara's life, this would become a familiar pattern: a succession of men, paper at the ready, would sketch as much of her as they were able; the hasty movements of chalk or pencil seeking to capture the texture of skin, the proportion of body parts, the elusive character of the subject – all to be transferred to oil on canvas or reproduced in clay. Whether the artist was Dutch or French or Venetian, one thing remained reassuringly constant from Clara's point of view: an abundant supply of food. However we finally judge Van der Meer, it is important to remember that he himself judged Clara's most basic and most necessary requirements absolutely right. No matter how much it cost him, Clara would have all that she could eat.

Looking at Wandelaar's rear view of Clara, then moving rapidly between it and the more familiar front view, it will be apparent that Wandelaar has taken great care to give the illusion that the rear view is separated from the front view only by a few moments – Clara has temporarily raised her head from the ground, the better to offset the skeletal model's ribcage. Yet the longer we look at the image, the harder it becomes to escape a growing conviction that Clara is the real subject of this extraordinary pair of engraved plates.

In the context of an anatomical atlas, front and rear views allow the reader to see a particular state of the human body in the round. Even as we look at the back of the skeleton, we realize that skeletons typically hold our attention from the front as we search the cavernous sockets of the eyes in a vain attempt to read what was once a face. Seen from behind, Clara's male companion is a shadow of even his skeletal self. The contrast between flesh and bone is now magnified beyond anything achieved in the conventional front view, as Clara's hind quarters dominate the viewer's visual field. And what Wandelaar strives to communicate – indeed, what seems to have intrigued him here more than the human body – is the unique arrangement and quality of the skin of the Indian rhinoceros.

It is hardly surprising that Wandelaar was fascinated by what he saw. To stand behind an Indian rhinoceros is to realize that it has a skin unlike any other animal's. Its hide has often been described as resembling armour plating, although this probably owes less to the startling reality than to impressions derived from Dürer's iconic engraving, which was made, incidentally, at a time when Dürer lived a few doors away from one of Nuremberg's armourers. Thick as the animal's skin obviously is, what strikes anyone looking at a mature Indian rhinoceros will not be its resemblance to the rigidity of metal but rather the fluidity of cloth.

When the seventeenth-century diarist John Evelyn saw a 'rhinoceros (or unicorn) being the first that I suppose was ever brought into England', his journal for 22 October 1684 goes on to record, 'Nothing was so extravagant as the skin of the beast, which hung down on her haunches, both behind and before to her knees, loose like so much coach leather, & not adhering at all to the body, which had another skin, so as one might take up this, as one would do a cloak or horse-cloth to a great depth, it adhering only at the upper parts.' What Evelyn attempts to describe is the realization that, close up, the ridge of the spine appears as a seam where clearly defined sections of skin meet and then flow over the flanks of the body. In some individuals, the skin develops huge folds that appear to hang off the body and over the tops of the legs: when such an animal moves at anything more than walking pace, this loose skin sways as though it is merely the covering of a smoother, more delicate animal underneath.

Trying to capture the sense that we are looking at an animal wearing an oversized skin, Hilaire Belloc in *The Bad Child's Book of Beasts* (1906) declares,

> Rhinoceros, your hide looks all undone.
> You do not take my fancy in the least:
> You have a horn where other brutes have none:
> Rhinoceros, you are an ugly beast.

The single horn referred to in Belloc's light-hearted verse is prominent in whimsical drawings accompanying his text: whether or not Belloc understood that only the Indian rhinoceros has such an 'undone' skin, his illustrations none the less clearly show the draping hide peculiar to this species, and also a refreshing lack of confusion between the one-horned Indian and two-horned African rhino. Though Clara's skin was not yet 'all undone' – that is, not fully developed when Wandelaar engraved her image – he must nevertheless have been conscious of the extraordinary characteristics it was already starting to exhibit; of the peculiarity of the tail's emergence from the well-defined seam of the spine; of the fact that he could easily do what the great Dürer could not – reach out and touch the object of his art.

In the *Just-So Stories* (1901), Rudyard Kipling recognizes that the Indian rhino's skin is striking not only on account of its massive folds but because the whole hide is peppered with what look like taut, irregular swellings, ready to burst through the surface. Kipling's 'How the Rhinoceros got his

Skin' imagines a single-horned Indian rhinoceros who must remove his *smooth* skin before he can take a dip in the sea. Whilst he is bathing near the beach of Altogether Uninhabited Island, the mischievous Pestonjee Bomonjee works 'cake crumbs and burned currants' into the skin that awaits the naked swimmer on shore. By the time the unfortunate Strorks has dressed and started rubbing his mysterious irritation it is too late: the 'burned currants' are well and truly part of his body.

Belloc and Kipling were writing within five years of each other at the beginning of the twentieth century and yet still found the skin of the species remarkable enough to comment upon. The wonder of Clara's eighteenth-century audiences therefore seems less remote, and the extent of Wandelaar's achievement becomes clearer. Trying to convey the texture of the skin in his engraving, Wandelaar opts for a series of discs that hint at surface irregularity. Moving from front to rear views of Clara, we see his confident delineation of the features of the hide in the rear view. Not only are these engravings the first anatomically correct illustrations of the Indian rhinoceros in Western art, they also perform the function of a sophisticated advertising campaign in that they challenge the viewer to go and test the truth of Wandelaar's unfamiliar representation by the simple expedient of paying an entrance fee. But just what preconceptions did Clara's early viewers approach her with, and where did most of their ideas about such exotic flora and fauna come from?

Wandelaar's pictures of Clara mounted a radical challenge to accepted ideas about the rhinoceros. Yet the majority of those who paid their hard-earned money to see Clara would have had no conception of Dürer's woodcut. They would, however, have had a great deal of knowledge about animals mentioned in the Bible. So to see Wandelaar as a pretender to Dürer's crown is only half the story: to the godly citizens of Leiden, any image of a creature mentioned in the Bible was expected to accord with the word of Scripture. To challenge Dürer was as nothing compared to a challenge to the Old Testament.

There are at least six and perhaps as many as nine references to the rhinoceros in the Bible, depending on which translation is preferred. Together with the writings of Roman authors, biblical verses were responsible for everything that was believed about the species until the early sixteenth century. Whereas classical Roman texts tend to focus upon facts about the behaviour of the animal (largely from observations made in the gladiatorial arena), biblical texts and commentaries emphasize qualities that the rhinoceros is thought to embody. So the Roman writer Pliny reports in his *Natural History* that the rhinoceros and the elephant are mortal enemies, and will not lose any opportunity to fight one another: this was a wholly false belief, but one that Pope Leo X had none the less intended putting to the test in the Papal gardens, had the rhinoceros sent to him by King Manuel of Portugal in 1516 not been shipwrecked and lost on its way to Rome.

This interest in the habits of the species may be contrasted with the very different focus of a theologian seeking to explain the reason for the divine creation of such an animal: according to the Venerable Bede, God makes 'fierce and poisonous animals . . . for terrifying man (because God foresaw that he would sin)'. Where Pliny wishes to understand how the rhinoceros relates to other animals, Bede wants us to appreciate how certain animals help man relate to God. In either case, the rhinoceros emerges as naturally aggressive (which may explain why Clara's illustrators repeatedly seem to take delight in showing her as placid and approachable). And it is this supposed aggression combined with a sense of unstoppable power that typifies Old Testament references to the creature. From AD 400 to 1400 the standard text of the Bible, the Latin Vulgate, used the rhinoceros as a symbol of unbridled power: 'God brought them out of Egypt; he hath as it were the strength of a rhinoceros' (Numbers 23:22); 'He hath as it were the strength of a rhinoceros: he shall eat up the nations his enemies, and shall break their bones, and pierce them through with his arrows' (Numbers 24:8); 'His horns are like the horns of the rhinoceros: with them he shall push the people together to the ends of the earth'; (Deuteronomy 33:17); 'Will the rhinoceros be willing to serve thee, or abide by thy crib? Canst thou bind the rhinoceros with his band in the furrow? Or will he harrow the valleys after thee? Wilt thou trust him, because his strength is great?' (Job 39: 9–11). If these verses look and sound somewhat strange, it may well be because most of us are rather more familiar with the language of the King James Bible and its immediate successors, all of which change the 'rhinoceros' of the Vulgate into a unicorn. Looking at Wandelaar's engraving, it is hard to imagine any confusion arising between a live rhinoceros and the mythical unicorn. Yet this is precisely what a number of writers from the thirteenth to the eighteenth centuries believed must have happened in order to give rise to a rich fund of unicorn lore. So how does an Indian rhinoceros evolve into a unicorn?

Modern attempts to explain our ancestors' beliefs in a variety of mythical animals often assume that there is a rational explanation for the stories told about a non-existent creature: the seductive charms of the stereotypical mermaid are replaced by the underwater songs of the manatee, and even sailors astute enough to work the complex rigging of a sailing ship become, through such rationalizations, simply confused about the difference between seductresses and sea cows. This search for rational explanations of myths is nothing new. When the Venetian traveller Marco Polo saw a live rhinoceros in Asia in the late thirteenth century, he supposed that the species must be the origin of the myth of the unicorn. Certainly, there is a great deal of similarity in stories told about the two animals. Gesner's influential *History of Four-Footed Beasts* (1658) sees the capture of a rhinoceros as being a straightforward matter for unicorn hunters armed with appropriate bait, and tries to reinforce the authority of his text with reference to earlier writers who are all agreed on the subject: 'He is taken by the same means that the *Unicorn* is taken, for it is said by *Albertus*, *Isidorus*, and *Alunnus*, that above all other creatures they love Virgins, and that unto them they will come be they never so wilde, and fall asleep before them, so being asleep, they are easily taken and carried away.' Where Gesner's seventeenth-century natural history endows the rhinoceros with the behavioural traits ascribed to the mythical unicorn, the Jewish Talmud credits the unicorn with powers traditionally associated with the rhinoceros, stating that the unicorn is capable of killing the elephant with a single belly wound inflicted by its fabulous horn.

Whatever the origins of the myths of the unicorn, the biblical scholars who produced the King James Bible had read just enough to begin to worry whether the three-ton Indian rhinoceros was a fitting symbol of the terrifying beauty or strength of divine power. Both Marco Polo's account of seeing rhinoceroses in his travels outside Europe and reports of the animal imported via Lisbon in 1515 – the inspiration of Dürer's woodcut – had suggested to biblical translators that the rhinoceros was no longer appropriate in this context. And so the rhinoceros of the Bible evolved into a unicorn which, like the awe-inspiring beasts of the apocalyptic Book of Revelations, is all the more fearsome for being not of this world.

To market Clara as the true unicorn was thus an option for Van der Meer, but one that he did not choose to pursue in any systematic way. Although a rhinoceros in the flesh proved most unlike a fictional unicorn, the Bible none the less afforded Van der Meer a unique marketing angle. As one of the earliest woodcuts of Clara announced to the inhabitants of Leipzig, 'there has now arrived a living rhinoceros, which many people believe to be the Behemoth, described in the Book of Job, chapter forty, verse ten'. One of the most enduring examples of faith in the Old Testament, Job is stripped of everything that he holds dear until, disease-ridden and despairing, he finally cries out for a divine explanation of the purpose that his suffering serves. Pointing Job to the most terrifying and powerful beasts that inhabit the land and sea – Behemoth and Leviathan, respectively – God demands that Job consider how little he truly understands of the world beyond its surface appearance: 'Behold now Behemoth, which I made with thee; he eateth grass as an ox' (Job 41:15). Indeed, Van der Meer's claim that Clara represented the Behemoth of the Old Testament would be the cause of intermittent theological debate provoked by her Tour, dividing those who believed they now had Behemoth in their midst from those who refused to equate one of the mysteries of the Bible with a creature they could reach out and touch even as she grazed in front of them.

Furthermore, Van der Meer was doubtless influenced by the contemporary Dutch fashion for arranging gentlemen's collections of 'curiosities' (preserved animal, vegetable and mineral specimens) in order that morally instructive lessons might be derived from them. The vogue for assembling cabinets of curiosities reached its high point in Europe in the seventeenth century, when an educated man might wish to demonstrate his interest in, and knowledge of, contemporary science by displaying as many curious specimens as he could acquire. Whether confined to a single display cabinet or occupying the entire wing of a stately home, such a collection was intended to demonstrate the latest understanding of the relationship between man and the natural world around him, ideally balancing man-made artefacts which we would today call archaeological or ethnographic objects with natural objects yielded up by both land and sea.

In the Dutch Republic in the seventeenth and eighteenth centuries, these *Wunderkamen* (or 'wonder cabinets') frequently moved beyond the purposes of aesthetic and educational display to act as three-dimensional stages for moral lessons – a child skeleton poised to play a miniature violin demonstrating, albeit in a disturbing fashion, both the transience of an individual life and the relative immortality granted by the creative arts. In advertising Clara as a living specimen of the animal that some theologians believed to be the Behemoth mentioned in Job, Van der

Meer targeted those members of Clara's viewing public who were used to looking for moral lessons in the world around them. As Clara grazed, some of those watching her would have been acutely conscious that here before them was a living, breathing illustration of one of the lessons that Job's story has to teach: to see Behemoth in the flesh only serves to reinforce how little is understood of the creature's true nature and purpose.

Even without her leaving Leiden, Clara's manifold appeal was apparent. Educated gentlemen and writers well versed in Greek and Roman paid to gaze on her and consider the truth of classical observations for themselves. Those whose reading was more often than not the Bible could wonder that anyone might have confused Behemoth with the unicorn, whilst those who believed that scientific enquiry had consigned both Behemoth and the unicorn to the realms of fable could nevertheless marvel at Clara's physical being and her natural behaviour. And among the gentlemen scholars, the theologians and the philosophers, there mingled those who were simply curious to see Van der Meer's astonishing creature, knowing that no one in their lifetime had seen a rhinoceros on mainland Europe before.

Eating grass just as Behemoth was supposed to do, Clara continued to increase in bulk and to become habituated to the presence of Van der Meer. Not only had the Dutch sea captain brought a live rhinoceros to Europe, but he was also succeeding in keeping her alive in captivity, as no one had done for over a thousand years. Even supposing an insatiable curiosity on the part of the citizens of Leiden to continue to pay to see Clara as she grew, Van der Meer had not, however, lost sight of his original plan: to display Clara across Europe, where the curiosity of its crowned heads and craftsmen would be more lucrative than the best rewards that Leiden alone could offer. The only difficulty that remained to be overcome was how best to transport a fully grown, three-ton Indian rhinoceros the length and breadth of Europe.

CHAPTER 3

To Entertain an Empress – Taking the Holy Roman Road

'Modern natural philosophers . . . have found God in
the folds of the skin of the rhinoceros.'

Voltaire, *Philosophical Dictionary* (1764)

There may seem to have been an obvious solution to the
difficulties of moving Clara around Europe: surely
she could have been made to walk. This, after all, was how
an elephant was taken from the French port of Lorient to
Versailles in 1772 and it is known that the animal and its
keeper took six weeks to make the 250-mile journey on
foot. But this most economical means of moving an
elephant was the brainchild of a French naval minister
responsible for overseeing the transportation of a creature
in which he had no financial interest (and one which the
king anyway regarded as a present, therefore not liable to

incur any cost beyond that of its maintenance in the royal menagerie). If the elephant suffered *en route*, or subsequently died as a result of its exertions, the minister (and his king) lost nothing.

As it was, Van der Meer's situation in the 1740s was very different to that of any other European private citizen who had ever contemplated the transportation of a large, exotic animal, for the Dutch sea captain was not merely the agent of one prince or governor hoping to gain favour with another ruler through some ostentatious gift-giving. Van der Meer had bought Clara in India and provisioned her at his own expense on the six-month voyage home, sinking everything into his investment. Given that she had survived a lengthy sea voyage and continued in apparent good health, Van der Meer did not wish to do anything to jeopardize Clara's long-term prospects. A large animal could be made to travel under its own steam on perhaps a single journey, but this could never be a way of life. Why would people pay for admittance to a barn or stable to see an animal that they could see for free as it walked, increasingly exhausted, from one town to another? For Clara's first journey beyond the borders of the Dutch republic, Van der Meer had to design and oversee the building of a travelling coach unlike any other. While the European aristocracy customarily favoured for their travels the lightest carriage bodies consistent with both elegance and status, Clara's weight and size demanded the heaviest vehicle ever built for a lady of the Grand Tour.

Had Van der Meer left behind a journal, generations of readers could have looked over his shoulder as he wrestled with the practicalities of owning and transporting the heaviest land animal on the planet. The nature of his problems can be gauged, however, from an account of the attempted transportation of a rhinoceros within France in 1770. For a single journey transporting a male rhinoceros from Lorient to Versailles, the French government paid for two days of work by carpenters, thirty-six by locksmiths, fifty-seven by blacksmiths and seventy-two by a team of wheelwrights. (Despite all this, the resulting wagon still collapsed *en route* and many more man hours were required to get the male rhinoceros back on the road.) The mere two days for the carpenters and the seventy-two for the wheelwrights indicate the heart of the problem: it is relatively easy to build a sturdy wooden crate in which to house a rhinoceros, but it is extremely difficult to secure the combined weight of crate and live contents on wooden wheels that will stand up to the rigours of the eighteenth-century road. Unlike the French government in 1770, Van der Meer could not afford to pay teams of smiths and wheelwrights, and yet he needed their skills to engineer a travelling loose box unlike any other.

A single image of his solution survives. The anonymous Venetian painting, *The Rhinoceros in its Booth* (painted around 1750–51 and now owned by the Banca Cattolica del Veneto, Vincenza), reveals much about aspects of Clara's public display but the canvas is unique among known images of her in its depiction of the vehicle used to move her the length and breadth of Europe for nearly twenty years. In the centre of the painting, Clara stands in the middle of a wooden enclosure, returning the stare of a gentleman seen to the viewer's left, who peers through an eye-piece. Behind him, a huge vehicle is parked, of such an idiosyncratic design that it is very obviously not a touring carriage of the aristocracy. At first sight, the long, low and crudely constructed box appears to have little to recommend it as the means of transporting a live animal, yet on closer inspection the canvas offers a wealth of detail about Van der Meer's ingenuity and care for Clara.

That the viewer is looking at the left side and rear wall of Clara's loose box is apparent from the absence on the body of the vehicle of a visible seat, or any hint of the shafts to which the horse team would have been attached. The back wall of the vehicle has a horizontal batten at its mid-point, but lacks any similar battening at its top. It therefore seems reasonable to assume that the rear wall of the wagon dropped to provide a reinforced entrance ramp, much like a modern horse box. The only visible window appears mean: more a reflection, perhaps, of Van der Meer's wish to avoid giving free viewings of Clara than a source of adequate light and ventilation. But if the vehicle's construction prevented casual sightings of Clara, it also protected her: she was prevented from seeing any potentially distressing movements outside.

The most remarkable feature of the whole is the size of the wheels. They are larger than those of any conventional carriage, and the anonymous artist flecks the outer rim nearest to the viewer with lighter paint, suggesting that the wooden spokes were bounded by an iron rim. The representation of the wheels as at least half the height of the wagon is explained only partially by their extraordinary size: they dominate any view of the side of the wagon because the body itself is unusually low-slung, implying that the chassis was placed directly on the axles and that there was no sort of suspension mechanism in between. We might imagine Clara rumbling across thousands of miles of established coaching routes, registering every pothole and rut along the way. But Van der Meer would have shared every bone-shaking jolt with her, and their experience was little different to that of the majority of travellers before the nineteenth century brought improvements in coach suspension and even a semblance of comfort.

Clara's itinerary and how long she stayed in any single location were largely determined by the number (and wealth) of potential viewers. But she also needed adequate time to recover from the stresses of travel, and her irritability at certain stages of her hormonal cycle had always to be taken into account. Her journeys therefore had to be

47

staggered, something Van der Meer was always careful to arrange. And such care clearly extended to the construction of Clara's coach. That it is never once recorded as bursting apart or collapsing under the considerable weight of its occupant is a testament to both its design and its builders.

Van der Meer's first calling of sea captain may well explain how his vehicle endured where the more expensive effort of a later French government failed. Before he had ever hoped to make his fortune through Clara's display, Van der Meer had worked for the powerful Dutch East India Company, and one of his responsibilities as a captain would have been the direction of carpenters and smiths regarding vital repairs should his ship have got into difficulty at sea, miles from the nearest friendly port. Moving between Leiden and Amsterdam in the early 1740s, Van der Meer knew where to find the craftsmen who regularly worked with heavy and complex masts and timbers, and who were used to making allowance for the violent tropical storms and other hazards of sea travel. As a captain, he had also been able to place regular ship's maintenance work where he chose; to hire and fire men; to promote them and recommend them for future commissions. A ship's captain made enemies, of course, but he also knew many who owed him favours. As a result, Van der Meer must have found it relatively straightforward to get Clara's travelling carriage built to his own exacting specifications.

Once confident that he could transport Clara outside the borders of the Dutch republic, Van der Meer then had to decide upon the best means of promoting both his and her long-term interests. A more hesitant man might have thought to begin their travels modestly, but Van der Meer must have been acutely aware that no one in living memory had managed to keep a rhinoceros alive on European soil. What if Clara should grow sick and die, or what if Van der Meer be left only with the revenue from provincial towns and country fairs? He would therefore capitalize on Clara's present health in one of the most audacious promotional tours ever staged, taking Clara all the way from Leiden to Vienna with the aim of attracting the attention of the Empress Maria Theresa, the power behind the greatest imperial dynasty in Europe.

If the precise route from Leiden to Vienna was largely pre-determined by Van der Meer's need to keep Clara's wagon on the best-maintained coaching roads, he was fortunate that the route also implied acquiescence to a political and national pecking order at which few would be likely to take offence. In the mid-eighteenth century, Germany was a collection of 350 sovereign states, ranging in size from relatively large regions such as Hanover in the north and Bavaria in the south to small ecclesiastical principalities such as Cologne or Mainz whose rulers controlled a very limited area. All in theory owed their allegiance to the Holy Roman Emperor, a title first

GLYNIS RIDLEY

conferred by Pope Leo X upon the warlord Charlemagne
in AD 800, and elevation to which was subsequently determined by nine electors representing the states of Bavaria,
Bohemia, Brandenburg, Cologne, Hanover, Mainz, the
Palatinate, Saxony and Trier.

Originally intended to designate the military champion
of the Catholic Church, the title of Holy Roman Emperor
had, since the fifteenth century, been seen as the natural
birthright of the male head of the Austrian Habsburg
dynasty. When the Habsburg family sought to occupy the
Spanish throne, Protestant Europe quaked at its uniting of
Church sanction with naked imperial ambition. From the
sixteenth to the eighteenth centuries, a succession of
European wars were fought to keep Habsburg power in
check, most notably the Wars of the Spanish Succession
(1702–13) and Austrian Succession (1740–48). In the 1740s,
the ranks of Habsburg subjects – Croats, Czechs, Germans,
Magyars, Serbs and Slovaks – were swelled by new acqui-
sitions in the southern Netherlands, Lombardy and other
Italian provinces.

As the Protestant Dutchman trundled Clara to Vienna, a
host of German rulers were necessarily courted along the
way, and were flattered to see the near-mythical rhinoceros
in advance of the Habsburg court. But Van der Meer made
it clear that Vienna would be his turning point on this particular journey and the Habsburg court therefore seemed to
be the journey's culmination. By the time he reached it,

this would be a court desperate for the novelty of the Dutch rhinoceros, reports of which would undoubtedly have reached Vienna. The gossip of ambassadors and the German nobility would be part of Van der Meer's advance publicity directed at the imperial family, but the chances of a favourable reception might also be increased by the fortuitous timing of his arrival in the Habsburg capital.

The title of Holy Roman Emperor, though long held by a Habsburg claimant, was technically an elected office and could be lost to the Habsburg family on the death of any incumbent. When the Emperor Charles VI realized that he would not leave a male heir, much imperial diplomacy was devoted to ensuring that all Habsburg dominions would be bound by a document known as the Pragmatic Sanction, which made provision for the succession of Charles's daughter, Maria Theresa, to all Habsburg crowns, titles and lands. But on Charles's death in 1740, signatories to the Sanction effectively declared it worthless as they instigated a most unholy scramble for power. The Elector of Bavaria, Charles Albert, was elected Emperor in 1741, though the legitimacy of the election was denied by both Maria Theresa and two additional claimants to the imperial crown: Philip V of Spain, who was not about to allow family ties stand in the way of huge territorial gains, and Augustus of Poland and Saxony, whose royal coffers sorely needed new sources of funding.

Meanwhile, Frederick the Great of Prussia saw a power

vacuum at the heart of Austro-Germany and invaded Silesia, threatening to take piecemeal what none of the imperial claimants could take whole. As mainland Europe descended into chaos, Britain and France weighed territorial considerations before attempting to tip the balance of power to their own advantages. Not until 1745 (and the death of Charles Albert of Bavaria, crowned Charles VII) would the Treaty of Dresden recognize Maria Theresa's husband, Francis I of Lorraine, as Holy Roman Emperor.

Planning as he was to arrive in Vienna in October or November 1746, Van der Meer was perhaps indulging in a little royal brinkmanship. He was bargaining on the fact that the imperial family would regard the culmination in the city of Clara's first European journey as some sort of recognition of renewed Habsburg pre-eminence, and that Maria Theresa and her consort, Francis I of Lorraine, would respond generously to anyone who so pleased the court. And if the courts of Germany could be made to start talking about the Dutch rhinoceros, then word would undoubtedly reach the imperial ear. But how could those courts be made interested in Clara's first tour? The minutiae of eighteenth-century European court etiquette varied from country to country, but was everywhere similar in its attempt to preserve the distance between rulers and ruled. Even the most autocratic of monarchs were pleased to leave the detail of everyday government to a range of ministers and it was the job of these ministers to be informed about what animated the man on the street, regardless of whether what interested him was talk of revolution or a rhinoceros.

Clara's first published appearance (in Wandelaar's engraving) had allowed Van der Meer to gauge the impact of a single well-placed and intriguing advertisement in his own home town of Leiden. He now determined upon the design and distribution of a series of posters and handbills, each specific to a particular area between Leiden and Vienna, and so skilfully conceived that Van der Meer could claim to be the originator of the first recognizably modern international advertising campaign. No German or Austrian alive in 1746 had had the chance to see a rhinoceros (unless a traveller had by chance seen the ill-fated London rhinoceros of 1739–41), but rhinomania was imminent and the sight of Clara would become *de rigueur* across all sectors of society.

Historical artefacts can present us with a paradox: disposable items that were produced and consumed in large quantities may survive in disproportionately small numbers compared to objects of high status. A mass-produced flyer designed to be stuck to buildings and left to disintegrate in the rain is less durable than a single image hanging on a gallery wall. The former will reach many of its contemporaries whilst the latter will remain for their descendants. Both types of images of Clara survive and it is highly probable that more variants on the twenty known broadsheet engravings remain to be discovered. That any of these ephemeral publications have survived at all, let alone so many different versions of Van der Meer's basic advertisement, may give some indication of the sheer range and scale of the advance publicity that Clara generated in 1746.

Looking at one of these broadsheet images, it is easiest to think of it in terms of a page of a modern newspaper, yet printed only on one side of the paper. Stuck to a wall, the image is eye-catching enough to make the passing pedestrian pause; folded up, the flyer can be taken home or to the tavern as a new talking point. Eighteenth-century society thrived on public spectacle and its accompanying visual and written record: those who gathered to see a hanging were prey to touts offering the supposed life story of the condemned, whilst slave traders, travelling salesmen and itinerant preachers have also left us examples of their publicity material. No matter if some of those confronted by a handbill had limited literacy or none: a graphic woodcut in a prominent position was generally good for business. The mass marketing of Clara would therefore place image above text, the bottom lines of which would promise the prospective viewer a sliding scale of admission charges that allowed everyone, no matter how humble, the chance to see a rhinoceros.

In all the versions of Van der Meer's poster campaign, the image of Clara remains basically the same, filling the top half of the page in an attempt to suggest her size, whilst

the texture and arrangement of her hide point to her difference from any other creature. Always she is shown
open-mouthed, as though ready to seize on whatever food
might present itself. Where a landscape is suggested there
is typically a palm tree or two, sometimes affording shelter
to one or more African natives with prominent bows and
arrows. (Even as the text proclaimed her Indian origins,
one non-European native was thought as good as another to
illustrate Clara's exoticism.) A small copper engraving in
the Rijksmuseum in Amsterdam shows an African warrior
taking aim at Clara from a small rise of ground, though
Clara herself strikes the same inquisitive and unthreatening pose in this version of the poster as she does in a variant
that survives in the Biblioteka Jagiellonska in Krakow: here
the African warrior has been replaced by a European sailor
whose ship rides in the background as he waves a beery
glass towards the open mouth asking, 'Clara, do you want a
sip?' Other variants on the basic theme show Clara in the
foreground of a desert landscape whilst in the background
another rhinoceros gores an elephant.

Two versions of the print (one in the British Museum
and one in private hands) show Douwemout Van der Meer
himself, ship's pennants streaming around him as he gazes
out over the printed text that summarizes his extraordinary
experience. Such images frequently displayed a prominent
eighteenth-century individual with the tools of his profes-
sion or interests. But this picture of Van der Meer inset into

the surrounding text is novel. The base of the picture's frame is a ship's hull, from which Van der Meer's bust rises. His coat and sash are those of a gentleman displaying honours bestowed upon him. His wig, shoulder-length and gently curled, is neither overtly elaborate nor especially plain. Together, wig and high forehead frame a gently rounded face from which two keen eyes refuse to meet the viewer's but instead stare off at some distant point on the high seas.

It is apparent from the various versions of the broadsheet that the image of Clara is virtually identical; only the text has evolved. On the woodcut made for Clara's 1746 tour of Austria and Germany, it is wholly in German. In the print surviving in the British Museum (which is known to have been in the collection of the naturalist Sir Joseph Banks), the text is shorter, allowing its replication in Latin, French, Dutch and English. As with the most successful modern advertising campaigns, the visuals and graphics move seamlessly between cultures whilst the text can be fine-tuned to allow for local difference. The text of the German woodcut shows just how Clara's story was spun to sell her first significant tour: it is lengthy, and it demonstrates how very shrewdly Van der Meer made his sales pitch to a wide social and intellectual spectrum.

The poster begins with an appeal to sentimentalists and readers of scripture alike: 'All animal lovers in Leipzig are informed of the arrival of a living rhinoceros, which many believe to be the Behemoth of the Book of Job, chapter forty, verse ten.' Since mid-eighteenth-century Europe was in thrall to what many social commentators saw as a pernicious fashion for very public declarations of intense emotional engagement with the world – the vogue of sensibility – the appeal to 'all animal lovers' is pitched at those who saw social mileage to be gained from an ostentatious display of concern for Clara's welfare. Those with a more serious purpose, however, are equally welcome: the unrelated second half of the sentence assuring Germany's large swathes of Calvinists that their visit will be theologically instructive. Which minister could blame his flock for availing themselves of the chance to see Behemoth? The poster goes on to insist: 'It is worth seeing by all who care to visit it. It is the first animal of this species seen in this town; it is about eight years old, and therefore still a calf, for it will continue to grow for many years, since these animals may live to be one hundred years old.'

Clara is here made novel on two counts: as the first of her kind to be seen in that place and as a Methuselah of the animal kingdom. (Captive rhinoceroses may live for up to forty years, but Van der Meer genuinely seems to have believed this more dramatic aspect of his own publicity – and since no European had any experience that could contradict the claim, it cannot be seen as deliberately deceitful.) From public weighings, the next information offered was unassailable: 'It is nearly 5,000 pounds in weight, and much larger and heavier than in 1741, when it was brought from Bengal to Holland by Captain Douwemout, not even three years old at the time.' To the average reader in Germany in 1746, the place name 'Bengal' would not have conjured up anywhere specific but a rather stereotypical sense of mysterious difference or 'otherness': an effect magnified by the succeeding claim that 'It was caught in Asia, in the realm of the Great Mogul, in the region of Assam, which is 4,000 miles distant from here'. Assam is to all intents and purposes another world, but one in which even the Great Mogul feels the reach of European trade.

A description of Clara then pours out in one single sentence, as though those who have seen her cannot contain their breathless excitement: 'This wonderful animal is dark-brown, like the elephant it has no hair, except for some hairs at the end of the tail; it has a horn on its nose, with which it can plough the ground much faster than a farmer with a plough; it can walk fast, and swim and dive in the water like a duck; its head is pointed at the front; the ears are like the ears of a donkey, and the eyes are very small compared to the size of the animal, only allowing it to look sideways; the skin looks as if it is covered with shells, overlapping each other, about two inches thick; the feet are short and thick, just like an elephant, but with three hoofs.'

The passage may seem laughable in places, but it reveals much about its intended audience. The assertion that the rhinoceros ploughs the ground with its horn is false in the agricultural context given, but it suggests that Van der Meer may have been wrongly interpreting an aspect of the behaviour of wild rhino which will temporarily lower their heads to whet their horns with mud or soil as part of the elaborate tussle for power between rival males during the mating season. Comparisons to a duck and a donkey usefully allow the reader to begin to picture what is unfamiliar through the glass of more familiar species. Yet, revealingly, Van der Meer must have felt confident that at least some of those who read the text had seen an elephant, or pictures of an elephant. Never absent from the European mainland as the rhinoceros had been from the third to the sixteenth centuries, the elephant was the most familiar of large, exotic animals. Clearly expecting a section of his audience to possess a classical education and to be schooled in Pliny's *Natural History*, Van der Meer then has the poster text repeat Pliny's wholly inaccurate account of the animosity of two species: 'The rhinoceros is the arch-enemy of the elephant, and when the two species meet, the rhinoceros tries to wound the elephant with his horn under the belly and kill it in that way.' What is intended here is both an appeal to classically educated gentlemen but also to those who hope that this exotic beast will be permanently spoiling for a fight.

A careless typographical error follows, making Clara male, as the reader is overwhelmed with the enormity of the creature's appetite: 'For daily sustenance, he eats sixty pounds of hay and twenty pounds of bread, and he drinks fourteen buckets of water.' The nervous reader need, however, have nothing to fear from a visit to see Clara: 'It is tame as a lamb, because it was only one month old when it was caught after its mother had been killed with arrows by the black Indians. When the animal was very young, it walked around a dining room, even when ladies and gentlemen were eating, as a curiosity.' As a final flourish, the species is credited with mysterious healing powers: 'This animal secretes some potion, which has cured many people from sickness.' Tempting though it is to see such a claim as a shameless confidence trick, Van der Meer was merely repeating received wisdom. The imagined curative properties of the rhinoceros are alluded to in the coat of arms of the Society of Apothecaries of London, founded in 1617: above the coat stands a Dürer-inspired rhinoceros, and the motto is a quote from Ovid's *Metamorphoses* that translates as 'I am spoken of all over the world as the one who brings help'. Even now, as Africa's black rhino population is pushed ever closer to extinction by an illicit demand for rhinoceros horn in the markets of the Middle and Far East, this centuries-old belief in the curative powers of the animal is still very much with us.

The poem that completes the main text of the woodcut is less straightforward to translate, and to capture the rhyming couplets of the original whilst preserving the sense is almost impossible. Even if rendered in prose, the German text's pervasive sense of wonder becomes more elusive, though Clara's supposed role as a walking illustration of divine power is still apparent:

> So wonderful is God [as seen in] his creatures that one finds everywhere the Almighty's wise traces. Of so many thousands none is so great or small that his care cannot be seen. Consider this animal you see before you here and ask yourself, do you not strive to search by day and night for God's miraculous might in the book of nature; the eye stares in amazement, the mouth must freely admit. God is as almighty as he is wonderful! And this drives us to praise him, who can never be praised enough; especially when one can also add this: God made it so man can take delight in it.

Essentially, the poem suggests that staring at a rhinoceros is far from a frivolous waste of time and money, but is rather a chance to meditate on the wonder of divine creativity. Indeed, whoever looks at the poster is promised in Clara a reflection of their interests: the devout are reminded of Job's dumbness when confronted with the existence of Behemoth; the educated are offered a glimpse of the rare animal mentioned by Pliny; the working classes who have probably never travelled further than from the local countryside to town may now see a creature from the realms of the 'Great Mogul' 4,000 miles away; the plain curious of all classes may simply stand and stare as the wonderful animal, the like of which has never been seen before, eats its way through a prodigious quantity of food.

The text of the poster concludes on a more businesslike note: 'This animal can be seen from nine a.m. to twelve noon, and again from two p.m. to six p.m. in the afternoon. Persons of rank can pay what they wish: all others pay one Gulden or four Groschen, according to the view. Copies of this woodcut will be on sale at the same place for one Groschen. Also available are large engravings for half a guilder, while the small engravings with the Indian cost two Groschen. N.B. You are advised that the animal will only stay ten or twelve days in this town.'

Van der Meer's commercial acumen is apparent in every detail here. 'Persons of rank' could, of course, choose to pay a token sum upon entrance, but which provincial squire or doctor would, in full view of his neighbours, risk an appearance of penny-pinching? Which member of the minor aristocracy would not wish the assembly to hear the chink of coins from their purse? The likelihood is that many professionals liked to think themselves of status within their communities and gave more to see Clara than Van der Meer would have felt comfortable charging on a fixed scale of entrance fees. Meanwhile, working people could pay according to their desired view and could stay as long as they wished: as the crowds ebbed and flowed around Clara's temporary pen, there seems to be no record of anyone being moved on by Van der Meer's party. The longer people lingered, the greater the crowds outside became, and the more desirable it seemed for those who had not seen Clara to gain admittance.

Any modern exhibition is likely to lead the visitor into a gift shop brimming with tie-ins, and Van der Meer needed no lessons in this respect. As the poster promised, anyone paying to see Clara could purchase the woodcut that had perhaps first caught their attention, or a 'large engraving' or a 'small engraving with an Indian'. This promotional material also offered choice, according to people's inclination and the ability to pay. It was likely, then, as Van der Meer first enticed Clara into her wagon, probably with an abundance of fresh hay, that his bags were already filled with at least three versions of the poster and he was filled with optimism about the proceeds a tame rhinoceros might bring.

In the spring of 1746, Clara's wagon began making its laborious way from Leiden to Hanover, where a local chronicler reported a 'hideous animal of female gender' and one G. L. Scheitz executed a watercolour of 'The Dutch Rhinoceros in Hanover' (now in the Stadtarchiv, Hanover), proudly proclaiming it to be taken 'from the life'. It was a modest enough beginning, but Van der Meer's posters were already beginning to penetrate the cities that lay before them, working to personalize the 'hideous animal' and to interest people in seeing her for themselves.

When Clara stopped at the Spittelmarkt in Berlin in

April 1746, Van der Meer had the most extraordinary confirmation of the wonder she provoked as Frederick the
Great and the most prominent members of his court came
to see her. Frederick was notoriously averse to the trappings of royalty: he was generally painted in defiant martial
poses and he scorned to wear a crown or, like the French
kings at Versailles, to make his private rituals the centre of
carefully orchestrated ceremony. But he was also one of the
most autocratic rulers of eighteenth-century Europe,
supremely self-assured and disdainful not only of the great
unwashed but also of most of the aristocracy. As he wrote to
Voltaire in April 1759: 'Let us admit the truth: the arts and
philosophy extend only to the few; the vast mass, the common people and the bulk of the nobility, remain what
nature has made them, that is to say savage beasts.'

For such a man to descend upon the Spittlemarkt with
his entourage to view Clara was a breathtaking coup for
Van der Meer, especially as the court party found her out
among the fish stalls. Fish oil, of course, had become the
moisturizer of choice for all the rhino imported into
Europe. Other, more fragrant lubricants existed and were
used in the early cosmetics industries, but the size and
texture of an Indian rhinoceros's hide would hardly register the application of a small pot of some expensive
preparation. In contrast, fish oil was relatively cheap and
plentiful, and every time he caught its smell, especially at
the height of summer, Van der Meer must have had to

remind himself that the nauseating onslaught on his senses was still more bearable than its alternative: a significant drain on his wallet.

Frederick might have rejected the trappings of monarchy, but his court was doubtless resplendent in the latest fashions and surrounded by a cloud of powders and perfumes designed to keep a world of unpleasant odours at bay. But if the gorgeous silks of the women's dresses trailed in the detritus underfoot, no one is recorded as making any complaint and Frederick himself was delighted by the visit, publicly pressing twelve ducats upon Van der Meer on the occasion of his visit on 26 April, and giving a further tip of six ducats the following day. Where the king was pleased to show his favour, the attendant nobility would have found it prudent to follow. Clara had only to be her usually placid self, eating her way through the day, and Van der Meer made money.

If the circumstances of Frederick's viewing are surprising, his patronage of Clara is less so. When he wrote to Voltaire in February 1766 that 'If there is one man in a thousand who thinks, it is quite something', he undoubtedly believed himself to be that 'one man'. Though denied a traditional classical education by his overpowering father, Frederick nursed a lifelong reverence for anything or anyone that he considered important to the furtherance of knowledge or capable of bettering the human mind. His accession to the Prussian throne in 1740 had allowed him to

consider what practical steps he might take to support the
spread of Enlightenment thought in his kingdom and in
1744 this resulted in his revival of the Berlin Academy of
Sciences and Letters. Its expressed mission was to be 'the
cultivation of every interesting and useful aspect of the various branches of philosophy, mathematics, physics, natural
history, political and literary history, as well as literary
criticism'. Whilst Frederick is now most readily associated
with an aggressive military expansionism that transformed
Prussia into one of the most influential powers in European
politics, his nationalism did not extend to a belief in
German intellectual superiority. The presidency of the
newly revived Berlin Academy was offered by Frederick to
the French scientist and mathematician, Maupertuis, to
whom the unsuspecting Clara seemed to promise nothing
less than proof of the existence of God.

Though Maupertuis did not assume the presidency of
the Berlin Academy until May 1746 (and returned temporarily to France in June on learning of his father's death),
his own correspondence with Frederick places him at the
Prussian court, and at the ear of the king, as early as January
1746. Clara's visit to Berlin in April therefore coincided
with an unusually relaxed period in the scientist's life
when he enjoyed great prestige but had little responsibili-
ty and pursued whatever interested him among the
scientific debates being conducted across Europe. Like all
of the eighteenth-century French thinkers who styled

themselves '*philosophes*', Maupertuis saw no contradiction in using his own intellectual discipline of mathematics as a starting point for the exploration of historical and theological questions.

Ever since Isaac Newton had insisted that an eyeball could not come into being by chance (that is, that the complexity of the universe might be taken to imply the existence of an intelligent creator), late seventeenth-century and eighteenth-century thinkers had defined themselves in relation to their view of Newtonian theory. Some defended not only the notion of intelligent design, but also of a designer who regularly intervened in his creation; others were willing to accept that creation was the work of a supreme creator, but rejected any notion of divine intervention in the minutiae of the self-contained and self-regulating system once it had been brought into being. When the most famous of the *philosophes*, Voltaire, wished to elaborate on the entry on 'atheism' in his *Philosophical Dictionary*, he referred scornfully and very specifically to what he called 'Maupertuis's objection' to the atheists, claiming under this prominent sub-heading that his countryman had 'found God in the folds of the skin of the rhinoceros'.

As Clara was in Berlin in April 1746 and Maupertuis can be placed there from January to May of the same year, it seems safe to assume the mathematician whom Frederick held in such high esteem was a visitor to the fish market also, possibly on the fringes of the court party. At this point in his career, Maupertuis was formulating his 'principle of least action', best summarized as a belief that nature always takes the simplest and therefore most elegant route to achieve some mysterious purpose (a theory that Maupertuis tried to prove through mathematical formulae). In Maupertuis's theory, the rhinoceros appears as it does for a reason, and not as some accidental freak of nature. To Voltaire, there seemed to be a yawning chasm between acknowledgement of the unique design of an animal and proof that its design fulfilled some great divine purpose. Thus the most topical insult that he could think to level at Maupertuis was that the mathematician had found evidence for the existence of God in contemplating Clara's extraordinary hide.

Valuing Voltaire's friendship, but clearly valuing the memory of Clara and his Academy president more, Frederick would return Voltaire's draft of the article on 'atheism', submitted to the king for his comments in 1752 (a full twelve years before the *Philosophical Dictionary* was published), making the royal suggestion that all references to Maupertuis and Clara be cut. Though Voltaire was not in the habit of modifying his written work to appease others, Frederick was a man of considerable influence and the article as printed in the standard edition of Voltaire's works is without any reference to Clara's place in a continuing eighteenth-century theological debate.

Indeed, so strong was Frederick's defence of his Academy President and the two men's shared interest in Clara that, whilst Voltaire could not resist a return to baiting Maupertuis in his most famous satire, *Candide* (1759), he substituted a discussion of wholly fictitious red sheep for any reference to 'the skin of the rhinoceros'. In chapter twenty-two of *Candide*, we therefore read a barbed aside about 'a northern philosopher who uses the formula $A + B - C \div D$ to prove that the sheep of Eldorado have to be red'. Had it not been for Frederick's interest in Maupertuis and Clara, *Candide* might well have satirized the philosopher who used a mathematical formula to prove that the Indian rhinoceros could not have evolved in any other way.

But all this lay in the future. Clara's stay in Berlin had been a success by any standards and Van der Meer must have hoped that the interest shown by Frederick's court, together with a liberal advance distribution of broadsheets, would result in a constant stream of paying viewers representing all sections of society. That stream was necessary, since royalty rarely expected to pay for its own entertainment and Frederick's gift of eighteen ducats rather typified the attitude of a man who respected any opportunity to widen his horizons. If Clara was to generate a steady income for Van der Meer, she had to draw in the prosperous burghers and tradespeople whose numbers far outweighed those of the ruling classes.

From Berlin, Clara's wagon rolled on to Frankfurt in

August and then Breslau in September, where evidence of her wide appeal survives. In the diary of Johann Ernst Grassmeder, a humble gardener, we learn of the exceptionally bad weather experienced by the citizens of Breslau in September 1746, which confined Van der Meer to the town. A mid-eighteenth-century gardener, even one in the pay of a wealthy household, can have had little in the way of disposable income, but Clara's presence in any town presented the locals with an opportunity neither they nor even their grandchildren might ever have again. As a new variation in the text of Van der Meer's broadsheet fliers emphasized, she was the rhinoceros 'which many have thought apocryphal until now'.

As heavy rain turned the dirt roads to mud, Van der Meer could not risk either the wellbeing of Clara or her carefully constructed wagon. Should the heavy vehicle become stuck fast, it would require many more than its usual complement of eight horses to drag it free. But the enforced stay in Breslau at least gave time to ensure the party's arrival in Vienna would have the greatest possible impact, and here Van der Meer left no detail to chance. The basic woodcut of Clara was re-engraved to herald her arrival in Vienna, Van der Meer commissioning Elias Baeck of Augsburg – well known for engraving exotica, anything from Chinese motifs to dwarves – to picture the ever open-mouthed Clara beside an elaborately dressed swordsman with a conspicuous feather in his cap. Although there is nothing in the familiar text accompanying Baeck's engraving that explains the moustachioed figure, local reports indicate that Clara entered Vienna with an escort of eight swordsmen, one for each of the eight horses that pulled her wagon into the city. Since Clara did not habitually travel with such a large retinue, it is reasonable to assume that Van der Meer hired eight men for the sole purpose of staging this elaborate entrance. If so, he must have been confident that the wage bill would be more than met by the revenue generated. Like any visiting dignitary's, Clara's arrival would be a very public affair in order that Viennese society might prepare itself to make her acquaintance.

The stay in Vienna is remarkably well documented in the pages of the local paper, the *Wienerisches Diarium*, which could scarcely conceal its surprise at the unprecedented nature of what followed Clara's arrival on 30 October 1746. Entering the city on a Sunday, Van der Meer's party established itself in the Freyung, an open area in the heart of the city ringed by houses of the titled and the wealthy and a rather more salubrious venue for receiving visitors than a stinking fish market. Exclusive though the surrounding property was, it did not enjoy the imperial seal of approval, for the court was centred on the Schönbrunn Palace in the Viennese countryside, a deferential distance being preserved between rulers and ruled. But on Saturday 5 November 1746, the court came to the Freyung.

Most important among the party was the Empress Maria Theresa herself. Only twenty-nine, she was the centre of the ever-expanding imperial family (her youngest daughter would be Marie-Antoinette) and, when not preoccupied producing one of the sixteen Habsburg heirs, she exercised ruthless control over imperial foreign policy. Her many portraits do not show the most striking royal beauty of the age, or even the most gorgeously dressed, but to contemplate any of these paintings is to come face to face with the only woman who can truly claim to have ruled the Habsburg dynasty throughout the six and a half centuries it dominated central and eastern Europe – a dominance only ended by the assassination of the Archduke Franz Ferdinand in June 1914 and the ensuing First World War. Very much in the shadow of Maria Theresa was her husband, Francis I of Lorraine, whose mother Elizabeth Charlotte of Orleans completed the imperial triumvirate. For Van der Meer to be graced with one such visitor would have been astonishing: to receive and to please all three in the Freyung was a certain prelude to social and therefore financial success. On the basis of the surviving evidence, Clara delighted her Habsburg hosts beyond even Van der Meer's wildest hopes.

The local press reported that, after viewing Clara themselves, Maria Theresa, the Emperor and the Empress Dowager went directly to the Hofburg Palace, where the royal children, together with the Empress Elisabeth, wife of the late Emperor Charles VI, were accommodated. By its very nature, this arrangement suggests the maintenance of an emotional as well as a geographical distance between imperial parents and children, but what Maria Theresa had seen in the Freyung demanded to be shared with her young family.

In a miniature by the painter Jean-Etienne Liotard (now in a private collection in London), the two-year-old Archduke Karl Joseph sits facing us in a high-backed chair, his tiny hands resting on the pages of an open book in front of him. His left hand rests on its left page, in the middle of a text under the unmistakable heading '*Le Rhinocéros*'. (Sadly, the particulars of the remaining text are not distinct.) His right hand strokes the illustration that occupies the whole of the right-hand page: a one-horned (and therefore Indian) rhinoceros. As no child's picture book – or royal picture book – is known from the period that shows this configuration of image and text, the book is presumably Liotard's invention, his image capturing Karl Joseph not only as a prince of the Enlightenment, eager to absorb his lessons, but as an ordinary child fascinated by the wonderful animal that all of Vienna, including his mother, had been talking about.

Given that Clara was not available for public viewings on a daily basis following Maria Theresa's visit on 5 November, it is entirely possible that Karl Joseph was himself taken for one or more private viewings in the

Freyung in the days after his parents had seen Clara for themselves. If this was indeed the case, it is easy to set aside all that makes the Habsburgs seem cold or remote from us, and to imagine instead a husband and wife besieged by their children with demands to be taken to see the latest novelty. Yet there is more that can be inferred about the miniature and its production.

For an artist to gain a sitting with one of the royal children, the Empress herself must have commissioned the work. It is certainly of rare quality and, whilst the Indian rhinoceros in Karl Joseph's picture book is too small to be immediately recognizable as Clara, she can be the only source for the illustration that the little boy so jealously guards. If Liotard asked for even a couple of hours of uninterrupted time sketching Clara, Van der Meer would certainly have been recompensed for the time he could not put Clara on public display. And the miniature would have been another potent reminder to the Dutchman that a variety of artists might be interested in representing her. Although he cannot have known it at the time, through Wandelaar's engraving and Liotard's miniature, Van der Meer was becoming the *de facto* owner of copyright to images of Clara. Now she not only made money for him when viewers saw her face to face, but the reproduction of her image offered to make him even greater sums, as the porcelain industry of Meissen would soon demonstrate.

But before Van der Meer left Vienna, the imperial

74

family wished to signal their approval with more than just money – and in the correspondence of the English writer, dilettante and classical collector Sir Horace Walpole, the extent of Habsburg patronage of Van der Meer becomes apparent. Walpole's friend, Sir Horace Mann, British Minister in Florence, writes to him in March 1750, affecting an aristocratic world-weariness as he anticipates Clara's arrival: 'This place is so void of events that we have been forced to be entertained with a most shabby Tripoline ambassador whom people's curiosity led to see as much as it will the rhinoceros which we expect from Rome, where it is gone to the jubilee. This animal is to be recommended to me with its master, Vander Meer, whom the Emperor has made a Baron for the merit of the beast. You must not be surprised that a Baron de l'Empire should follow this trade, when we are told that Augustus himself did not disdain to be a *rhinocerontajo*, by showing one publicly to the Romans.'

From the meeting in the Freyung in November 1746, Van der Meer had gained an imperial title. It must have mattered little to him that the Holy Roman Empire of the 1740s was, as Voltaire famously remarked, neither holy, nor Roman, nor an Empire. The baronetcy bestowed by one of the most powerful Catholic figureheads in Europe upon the Protestant Dutch sea captain was of value not for the indeterminate status it conferred, but for the doors it opened. The Habsburg dynasty was married into Europe's most powerful courts, and where it lacked family interest, it maintained strong ambassadorial representation; its power reached across a continent. The Schönbrunn's inhabitants had bestowed interest and favour upon him, and Van der Meer understood enough of European politics to know that the continent's other courts were now accessible to him.

As for Clara, she continued eating and growing: the horn which is just beginning to show in Wandelaar's 1742 engraving was now prominent. Clara was everything that was expected of her, and her continued good health and growth suggest that life on the road was at least tolerable for her. As for Baron Van der Meer, it is safe to assume that, as he left Vienna on 26 November 1746, he could not remember a month like it and had a broad smile upon his face.

CHAPTER 4

Pretty in Porcelain –
The Muse of Meissen

'Meissen . . . is rendered impenetrable to any but those who
are immediately employed about the work . . . they are all confined as prisoners.'

Jonas Hanway, *An Historical Account of the British Trade
over the Caspian Sea* (1752)

From Vienna, Clara's wagon turned west, but whilst
Salzburg and Munich would seem obvious stopping
points, no firm evidence places Clara on view in either of
these cities. After the Austrian capital, she is next documented in early March 1747 in Regensburg, where one
J. M. Barth used the occasion of her visit to rush out a pamphlet proclaiming the rhinoceros to be the Behemoth of the
Old Testament: a position vigorously contested in an
immediate written riposte by the disputatious J. Reinhard.

Leaving the amateur theologians and natural historians of Regensburg to their quarrel, the wagon rolled on in early April 1747 to Freiberg, where the Wiesemann Inn benefited from a noticeable upturn in takings as large crowds came to see Clara for themselves. But after Vienna, Van der Meer had only one city in his sights: Dresden, where the court of the Elector of Saxony controlled the oldest and most lucrative of European porcelain factories.

The very notion of a rhinoceros trundling towards a porcelain factory seems to presage disaster. Yet in Meissen's workshops, Johann Joachim Kaendler would have welcomed the arrival of an entire menagerie, for the factory's – and arguably eighteenth-century Europe's – greatest animal modeller had never seen a rhinoceros. Generally credited as the man who invented collectable china figurines, Kaendler longed to see for himself the animals he yearned to immortalize in clay. As things stood, the only likeness available to him was a copy of Dürer's *Rhinoceros* of 1515, and Dürer had never seen the animal either. The conditions of Kaendler's employment only added to the difficulty of seeing a rhinoceros: he was a virtual prisoner at the Meissen factory. Yet Kaendler did see Clara during her stay at Dresden from 5 to 19 April 1747, and the sketches and resulting models that he made of her were to change for ever the way Europeans imagined the species and represented the rhinoceros in the plastic arts.

Porcelain is so readily available today that it is difficult to

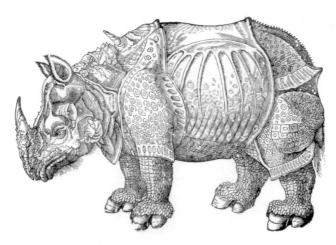

When Dürer engraved his *Rhinoceros* of 1515, he worked from a second-hand report. For over two hundred years afterwards, artists would reproduce variations on his engraving, showing the species with an entirely fictitious dorsal horn.

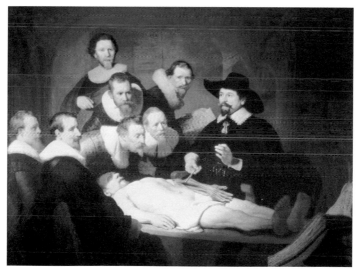

The Anatomy Lesson of Dr Tulp by Rembrandt Harmensz. van Rijn (1632).
Anatomists were guaranteed a good audience and their
books were eagerly sought after. Hence, no doubt, the popularity
of Wandelaar's engravings of Clara.

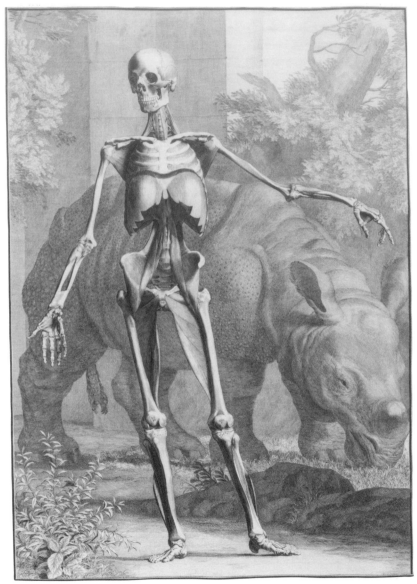

Promotional material for Clara's Tour often served a dual purpose.
Here, engravings by Jan Wandelaar advertise both Clara's presence in Leiden
and the forthcoming publication of a new medical textbook.

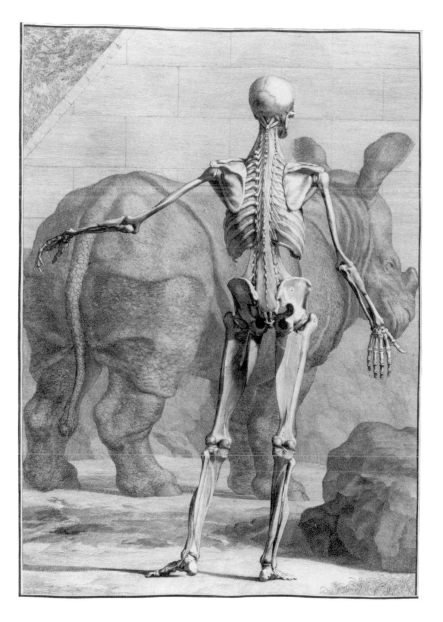

Illustrations on dinner services were expected to be interesting, varied and, preferably, exotic. In reproducing Dürer's *Rhinoceros*, Meissen's painters led aristrocratic diners into error. But when their chief modeller saw Clara in April 1747, the porcelain factory's representations of the animal were immediately changed.

One of five identical sculptures, this bronze suggests there was a demand for high-quality memorabilia of Clara. Through such artefacts, Van der Meer effectively established his copyright over images of Clara.

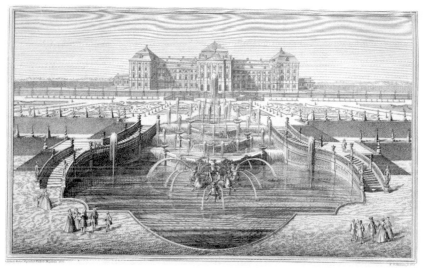

The elaborately landscaped gardens at Weissenstein, the seat of the Landgrave Frederick II of Hesse. Clara may well have grazed here in the summer of 1747.

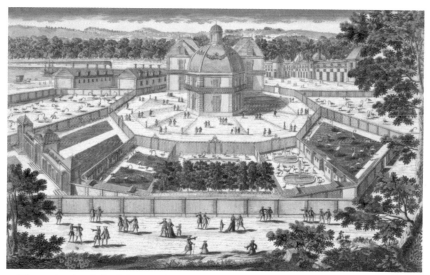

The animals of the Menagerie at Versailles were a demonstration of France's imperial reach, and had Louis XV not thought Clara's price too high, his zoo would have become her home in January 1749.

Clara influenced the French decorative arts as significantly
as she did Parisian culture. This exquisite ormulu clock is the work
of three leading craftsmen.

As Louis XV's favourite animal painter, Oudry was commissioned to produce a life-size oil painting of Clara during her stay at Versailles. It became the blueprint for smaller engravings which appeared in Diderot and D'Alembert's *Encyclopédie* and Buffon's *Histoire Naturelle*.

One of Canaletto's celebrated views of the Grand Canal in Venice. Van der Meer may well have encouraged rumours that Clara toppled from her barge into the waterway when she visited the city in January 1751.

Just who is on display in Pietro Longhi's *Exhibition of a Rhinoceros at Venice* (1751) – Clara or the young Venetian woman in the front row? Longhi painted two significantly different versions of this enigmatic picture for different patrons.

appreciate its rarity in Europe in the early eighteenth century. European traders had long admired the seemingly
flawless appearance of the strong yet sheer white vessels
and *objets d'art* offered to them at the Chinese imperial
court, but all attempts to replicate the quality of what they
saw ended in failure. Chinese workers could not be tempted
to assist European merchants in breaking the Chinese
monopoly on hard-paste porcelain, so European potters
struggled on in ignorance of its basic ingredients, the ratio
of those ingredients to each other, the temperature at
which any final mix should be fired and how long such
firing should last. Fields of European clay were dug
and mixed with a variety of compounds before Johann
Frederick Böttger finally pleased his master, Augustus the
Strong of Saxony, by demonstrating that kaolin (or china)
clay from a mine in Colditz, when mixed with alabaster and
fired for five hours, yielded a result not so far removed from
the Chinese porcelain that was Augustus's passion.

As Augustus had imprisoned Böttger in the
Albrechtsburg, a former royal palace in the town of
Meissen, it is not too much of an exaggeration to say that
the discovery of a workable formula for the production of
Meissen porcelain saved Böttger's life, just as it did the
economy of Saxony. If Augustus had trouble keeping
his hands to himself in the proximity of any attractive
woman at his court, he had even more difficulty resisting
the lure of brilliant, translucent Chinese porcelain, and his

79

addiction to acquiring it was bankrupting his kingdom. In the first year of his reign alone, 100,000 thalers were spent on porcelain for the royal collection and disappeared into the coffers of Chinese factories and their agents. (When Frederick the Great invaded Dresden in 1756, his privy councillor Schimmelmann found that the profits on re-selling 120,000 thalers' worth of porcelain allowed the purchase of a palace in the city, a castle in the country and a large estate in Denmark.)

Following Böttger's discovery, other Meissen employees refined their understanding of porcelain production so that, by the mid-1730s, over ninety workers were employed at the Albrechtsburg, producing exquisite porcelain that was sold across Europe, not to mention the 880,000 thalers' worth commandeered by Augustus himself. Once a drain on the Saxon economy, porcelain now became its key export, and Meissen had attracted the skills of modellers such as Johann Gottlob Kirchner and then Johann Kaendler. Was there anything that could not be replicated, life-sized, in porcelain?

Augustus had no time for the dreary details of kiln size or the difficulties of sustaining of temperatures in excess of 1,400°C. He wanted a new wing added on to the palace that he had inherited and in 1730 consisted of a central block and two flanking wings. A fourth side would create an internal courtyard. It was, Augustus directed, to be built entirely from porcelain, complete with its own porcelain

CLARA'S GRAND TOUR

menagerie on the upper floor: an intended 170 feet in length, the menagerie was to be populated with life-sized animals and birds made wholly from porcelain and painted to suggest their natural colours. Augustus would probably have eaten porcelain had a way been found to present it, although as he appears to have replaced the decaying royal teeth with a set of porcelain dentures, he achieved the next most palatable option.

Finding the skills of first Johann Gregor Herold and then Johann Gottlob Kirchner to be lacking when it came to creating the menagerie, Augustus did not pause to consider that, during Kirchner's residence, the factory seemed to have reached the technical limits of what could be produced. The fact remained, however, that the standard form of porcelain paste settled upon at Meissen would still fracture when moulded beyond the size of a table-top piece. With large fissures opening up in the firing process, even the enamellers' art could do little to disguise a series of deeply flawed models. When Kirchner, in his desperation, started frequenting the local inns and brothels more regularly than the Meissen workshop, Augustus installed as 'model master' Johann Joachim Kaendler, whose interest in the medium would lead him to succeed where others had failed.

Kaendler's first creations for the royal menagerie date from 1731: an eagle six and a half feet tall with outstretched wings, closely followed by two life-sized ospreys, an owl, a hawk and a heron, in addition to a larger than life St Peter for the royal chapel. With these creations, Kaendler established himself as the foremost exponent of porcelain modelling in Europe, and he now realized that even larger pieces might be made in sections, providing the manner of their construction was not obvious to the viewer. The scale of his achievement is astonishing. Few of the life-sized birds and animals he made and still survive are without random fissures that opened up on firing and cooling. But it is a testament to Kaendler's technical brilliance that these flaws scarcely detract from the impact of his wholly naturalistic sculptures. The impact of an entire menagerie would have been extraordinary.

The depiction of realistic animals is, however, an artistic as well as a technical challenge. Whereas examples of the birds he modelled could be found in the royal aviary, Kaendler had only one source for all of his preconceptions about the rhinoceros, and that was Dürer's 1515 archetype, copied with variation across Europe ever since. Indeed, the distinct armour-plated sections of Dürer's rhinoceros must have struck Kaendler as being particularly amenable to being reproduced in porcelain: each section could be reduplicated and then fired to become part of a larger model. So one can imagine his surprise at his first sight of Clara, a double-take hardening into a thoughtful stare as he realized that the Meissen factory had, for several years, been exporting wares that completely misrepresented the species. The shock may even have temporarily dampened his delight in being accorded the special privilege of being allowed to meet Van der Meer and Clara outside the factory prison. But when the Dutchman doubtless reminded him that Clara would only stay in Dresden for two weeks, Kaendler would have buried his incredulity in his sketch pad. Meissen ware may have previously been in error in its depiction of the rhinoceros, but from April 1747 onwards, this would be corrected. Clara would become the model for all Meissen representations of her kind.

The problem with Meissen representations of the rhinoceros prior to Clara's visit to Dresden is neatly illustrated by a dinner service now in the possession of the Duke of Northumberland and on display at Alnwick Castle. The dinner service is representative of those used to showcase the skills of Europe's burgeoning eighteenth-century porcelain industry: where Meissen had led the way in emulating Chinese wares, Sèvres and Chelsea followed. Grand porcelain dinner services were commissioned by all the crowned heads of Europe, and though Catherine the Great's Swan Service (in excess of a thousand pieces) was exceptional for its size, it was entirely typical in that no two designs painted under its glaze were the same. Whether the subject was landscapes, flowers or animals, no aristocratic diner expected to find that they and their neighbour were peering at the same illustration as one course succeeded another.

The Northumberland Meissen Service represents the rhinoceros not once, but twice, most strikingly at the centre of a large platter, where the animal is dwarfed by a riot of flowers and insects. Taken separately, neither the floral border nor the rhinoceros is comic, but when juxtaposed, the assault on the viewer's sense of scale is faintly ridiculous, the horn on the end of the animal's nose finding its mirror image in the petal of a mutant white carnation. And it is here that the inaccuracy of Dürer's conception is clearest, for the horn that is most obvious to the viewer is not the solitary horn of the Indian rhinoceros rising from above the nostrils, but the dorsal horn, protruding from above the front haunches.

In European ceramics, paintings and tapestries made prior to Clara's Tour, the legacy of Dürer is apparent in the presence of this second, entirely fictitious dorsal horn whenever the rhinoceros is represented. It can be seen, among other places, on a bronze door of Pisa Cathedral (School of Giovanni Bologna, c.1602), on a bronze medal carved for Alessandro de' Medici (by Anton Francesco Selvi, c.1740, now in the British Museum) and on a Gobelin tapestry panel from the monumental series Les Anciennes Indes (1708–10, the complete series being on display in the Palace of the Grand Master of the Order of St John in Valletta, Malta). Whatever the scale of the image or the medium of its execution, Dürer's Rhinoceros determined the European image of the animal for over two centuries –

and Clara, placid, affectionate, and conspicuously lacking in a dorsal horn, was everything that Dürer's rhinoceros was not.

To understand how Dürer came to credit the Indian rhinoceros with a second horn is to arrive at the heart of European preconceptions about the species. The animal that was the inspiration for Dürer's woodcut was the first rhinoceros to set foot on European shores since the third century. It arrived in the Tagus Estuary in May 1515, and its historic landing would be commemorated within two years as a stone rhinoceros was made one of the corbels on the Belem Tower that commands the estuary's edge. The adult rhinoceros was a gift from Muzafar II, the ruler of the Indian state of Gujarat, to Alfonso d'Albuquerque, Governor of Portugal's Indian territories, and a gift of such rarity that there was only one thing the governor could do with it: present it to his king, Manuel.

The Portuguese monarch in his turn decided he would present the rhinoceros to Pope Leo X, intending that it should both ingratiate him – and Portugal's colonial agenda – with the pontiff and trump whatever the Spanish might offer. Before parting with the animal, however, Manuel could not resist testing the truth of Pliny's assertion that the rhinoceros and the elephant were mortal enemies. The king had a small herd of elephants at his disposal and decreed combat on 3 June 1515, but far from rushing to gore its opponent, the rhinoceros seemed unmoved whilst the sacrificial elephant retreated as far as it could from its unfamiliar opponent. Manuel duly made arrangements to send the rhino on to Leo X, who had an elephant of his own (Hanno) and also hoped to stage a similar fight in the papal gardens. (Despite all evidence to the contrary, no educated man could quite believe that a great Roman writer such as Pliny might be in error.)

In December 1515, the rhinoceros was loaded on board ship in Lisbon. Surviving descriptions indicate that the animal had been adorned with a gilt-iron chain to restrain it and a collar to which were attached roses and carnations. The ornamental detail is particularly interesting, for Dürer's rhinoceros displays a strange floral excrescence behind the mouth at the point at which the massive head meets the body. The image is so often reprinted that we forget what we already know: rhinoceroses are not like this. They do not have flowers growing from their skin and no species of rhinoceros that has ever walked the earth has had the dorsal horn Dürer depicts. Yet his image has so insinuated itself into Western culture that the catalogue of an exhibition of Dürer's work staged at the British Museum in 2002 can refer to 'the fairly accurate image' that Dürer used to produce his sketch and, mystifyingly, to the fact that the 'beast is thought to be a now extinct species of Indian rhinoceros'. That no one has ever seen an Indian rhinoceros (or any other rhinoceros) quite like Dürer's creation has, however, nothing to do with extinction or bad craftsmanship on Dürer's part but everything to do with theatrical display.

When the ship carrying the Lisbon rhinoceros foundered off the Italian coast in January 1516 and the animal drowned, its likeness had already been sketched in Lisbon and reports made of its appearance on a stopover near Marseilles. Here Francis I of France and his queen inspected the rhinoceros and a mock-battle was staged around it for royal entertainment, with oranges taking the place of cannonballs. It is generally agreed that Dürer worked from a printed account of the animal that had found its way into the Nuremberg press, and much has been written on the proximity of Dürer's workshop to the armourer's quarter in Nuremberg, as though this accounts for the artist's predilection for the familiar contours of the armour plating that seem to encase the upper half of his creature. Yet the strong possibility exists that Dürer's *Rhinoceros* is a true representation of the animal – but as it was dressed for loading at Lisbon and its subsequent presentation to Francis I.

That the rhinoceros was festooned with flowers attached to the velvet overlay of a collar was documented by contemporary reports. That it was subsequently the centre of a mock-battle staged for the visiting French court is also recorded. Could it be that Dürer pictures the animal with a dorsal horn emerging from the clearly delineated plates of the hide because it had in fact been encased in armour presented as part of Muzafar's gift to Albuquerque? A weight of contemporary evidence lends support to this suggestion.

One of the finest surviving examples of a complete suit of horse armour from the early sixteenth century – the so-called Burgundian Bard presented by the Holy Roman Emperor Maximilian to the English king, Henry VIII – shows in its construction the exact configuration of armoured plates that is apparent in Dürer's engraving. This is particularly striking at the rear of the Burgundian Bard, where the armour appears to come to a clearly defined point as it protects the top of the horse's tail. A similar structure, resembling the dropped visor of a helmet, is very noticeable over the rear flanks of the rhinoceros in Dürer's engraving. Furthermore, the suggestion that the rhinoceros is pictured wearing a suit of mail is reinforced by examination of the faulds (the sections of plate covering the upper legs). The Burgundian Bard shows a similar degree of armoured protection afforded to the horse's upper body, while the legs themselves are freed from the cumbersome restrictions of armour.

Dürer's Nuremberg contemporary, Hans Burgkmair, who was also working from second-hand reports of the Lisbon rhinoceros, produced a 1515 woodcut of his own. Unlike Dürer, however, Burgkmair gives his viewers a realistic animal, minus prominent plating and dorsal horn. As both Dürer and Burgkmair worked from the same source, and Burgkmair's engraving is more naturalistic than Dürer's, neither man would appear to have been under any illusion about the true appearance of a rhinoceros. Dürer must therefore have embellished the creature's appearance for a reason. And finally, amongst the extensive collection of eastern armour and saddles in the National Museum of India, New Delhi, there are horse saddles with sharply angled pommels that can be held by a rider, if necessary. When the saddles are seen in profile, the pommels are stark ornamental projections, giving animal and rider an appearance of shared aggressiveness.

It is not incredible, then, to suppose that Dürer deliberately represented the Lisbon rhinoceros as though in armour, and that the contours of these protective plates were determined by those of contemporary European and Indian designs for horse armour. While Burgkmair engraves a realistic rhinoceros, Dürer offers an animal that says more about the accoutrements of kingship and war than about the nature of the species. What could be thought more appropriate for the presentation of the rhinoceros to first the French king and then the Pope than that its dark skin should be clothed in shining armour? Indeed, many copies of Dürer's image colour the upper body in shades of gold or terracotta, as though the real animal stands encased within.

In Dürer's lifetime and after his death, the woodcut was used in nine separate printings to generate an unknown number of prints. Disseminated across Europe, Dürer's *Rhinoceros* was the template for all representations of the species from 1515 until the eighteenth century. In fact, before Clara arrived in Dresden and before Johann Kaendler took over as Meissen's master modeller, Johann Kirchner had fired a 'rhinoceros after Dürer' (1731–4) showing the animal with its head lowered and a prominent dorsal horn facing forward, ready to do battle. But as Kaendler studied Clara, she appeared as far removed from the Dürer image as it was possible for her to be. It was fortunate that he was ambitious in his work, for a necessary consequence of his modelling of Clara was that Meissen ware would now challenge the European image of the rhinoceros that the factory had itself only recently been promoting. Even so, the correction of impressions held about the species through the manufacture of a range of *objets d'art* was as nothing when compared to the technical difficulties of firing a large porcelain animal. Where Van der Meer had wrestled with the practical difficulties of getting Clara on the road, Kaendler now puzzled over how best to turn her into art.

As Clara was in Dresden for only two weeks from 5 to 19 April 1747, Kaendler must have sketched her from as many angles as possible, just as he had sketched the birds in the King's menagerie. Of course, as Van der Meer controlled access to Clara and therefore the copyright to her image, Kaendler's expenses for April 1747 included fees paid for the privilege of sitting and sketching her, undisturbed, as she ate and slept. Once her wagon had rumbled on to the annual Easter fair at Leipzig, Kaendler would have only his drawings from which to recreate a three-dimensional creature.

Among the acknowledged results of Kaendler's work are a Meissen sculpture of a seated mandarin and rhinoceros under a palm tree, complete by 1750 (now in Frankfurt), and the sculpture *A Turk Riding a Rhinoceros* of 1752 (now in Bern). Both groups of figures appear in the standard literature on Meissen ware of the period as illustrative of Kaendler's reign as model master and both have much to teach us about enduring cultural stereotypes. No species of rhinoceros has roamed either China or Turkey since pre-historic times, yet these exquisitely modelled porcelain groups draw upon a lexicon of 'exotic' clothing (the mandarin wears a full-length purple robe, while the Turk sports slippers, flowing trousers and a turban) to suggest a fabled Orient where it would not be unusual to find a creature so alien to Europe as the rhinoceros. No doubt these two pieces were prominent in the factory's display of its latest wares and caught the eye of a wealthy shopper at one of the many trade fairs where such pieces were displayed. Taken separately, both porcelain and the Dutch rhinoceros were talking points for the fashionable world: brought together, the combination was irresistible.

There remains, however, a group of German models of Clara of an altogether different nature, yet their construction suggests that they, too, are the work of Kaendler. The bronze rhinoceros now owned by the Barber Institute of the University of Birmingham is of mysterious provenance. It is generally agreed that the Berlin museum director, Wilhelm Bode, who pronounced it to be 'one of the best animal bronzes of the Renaissance', was uncharacteristically wide of the chronological mark. Renaissance artists derived their idea of the rhinoceros from Dürer's armour-clad archetype, complete with its fictitious dorsal horn. In contrast, the Barber bronze is entirely naturalistic. In textbooks and the Barber Institute's own literature, it is usually recorded as German, dating from approximately 1750. The bronze is in every detail identical to a white marble rhinoceros in the collection of the Bowes Museum (at Barnard Castle, Durham), where the sparse information available on the sculpture suggests that it may be German or French and dates from approximately 1750.

It is not simply that Clara adopts an identical stance in each of her marble and bronze guises. In fact, the two sculptures differ only in the material of their construction. Furthermore, giving either one or both anything more than the passing glance they habitually receive from museum visitors will convince the viewer that these sculptures are based on an individual animal with a distinct character: this is Clara, scaled down, perhaps, but Clara nevertheless.

The marble sculpture is one of a kind. Three examples of the bronze are known: at the Barber Institute in Birmingham; in the Victoria and Albert Museum in London (Salting Collection); and in the Louvre in

Paris (Heseltine and Madame de Behague collections). The model then presents again itself in another medium: as the support of a Frankenthal porcelain clock (now in Munich), where a porcelain drape added over the middle of the back includes the representation of an turban- and earring-wearing African head. (Eighteenth-century Europeans decorators and viewers appear to have regarded the pairing of interchangeable and stereotypical African, Indian and Turkish figures with figures of Clara as an appropriate means of representing a vague conception of 'the East'.)

The same model of Clara therefore appears in marble, bronze and porcelain manifestations, and the nature of the three media allows the sequence of the models' production to be deduced. Marble cannot be cast like molten metal: the marble statue in the Bowes Museum is therefore an original sculpture and the first in the sequence. Marble statues can, however, be used as the basis for metal casts. Smothered in plaster of Paris, a marble statue can be used to form a hollow mould into which molten metal can be poured. The same plaster of Paris mould, or a new mould generated from a bronze, could also be filled with porcelain paste. In fact, the Frankenthal porcelain model of Clara that supports a clock shows precisely the degree of shrinkage that would be expected by the firing of a porcelain cast in a mould made from the bronze or marble versions of the sculpture.

That this model was replicated across three distinct media says much about contemporary satisfaction with its naturalism, and also reveals a strong demand for this image of Clara. Van der Meer did not commission such items out of his own pocket and then hope to find a buyer: the marble original was surely made with an awareness that it could be used as a pattern from which to generate other models, and there was clearly sufficient market interest to suggest that such models would not remain unsold. The woodcut and copper-engraved posters that Van der Meer offered for sale wherever Clara stopped were simply not enough to satisfy public demand. Wealthy Germans wanted Clara memorabilia of high status, fit to be put on display.

Kaendler's forte was the table-top figurine, it is true, but the marble, bronze and porcelain models of Clara from this period with an accepted German provenance are emphatically the work of an exceptional animal modeller. The naturalism of the Barber bronze is evidence of this. Kaendler had originally been brought into the Meissen factory to fulfil Augustus the Strong's wish for a life-sized porcelain menagerie and had thought to obviate the problems inherent in firing large pieces by producing them in carefully disguised sections. But why should production of a model somewhere between the scale miniature and the life-sized not have appealed to someone with his insatiable modelling appetite? In the absence of a more obvious candidate, Kaendler remains the most likely originator of the model sequence that survives in Europe's museums today.

Before Clara left Dresden, the heir of Augustus the Strong, Augustus III, Elector of Saxony and King of Poland, requested a private viewing of her and, like Maria Theresa before him, he brought his ailing son with him: a rhinoceros was clearly regarded as an edifying and instructive sight for the crowned princes and princesses of Europe. Had Clara had been given to bouts of aggressive or unpredictable behaviour, she would never have been placed within reach of the assembled heirs of any royal house – and the frequency of her royal visitors, of all ages, is powerful proof of her gentle and unthreatening nature. In a world where monarchs could command practically anything they wished, a tame rhinoceros was still the rarest of sights and even the most authoritarian ruler could feel justified in letting their wonder show. The royal visit on 19 April was judged a great success, as the heir apparent was pleased with the occasion, and Augustus doubtless showed his gratitude to Van der Meer for causing the Electoral Prince to show interest in something beyond his own feeble condition.

From Dresden, Clara's wagon took four days to reach Leipzig. Timing was all-important at this stage in the journey, for Van der Meer wished Clara's stay in the town to coincide with the annual Easter fair that drew both wealthy city dwellers and crowds from the surrounding countryside. To other stallholders at the fair, the presence of the Dutch rhinoceros was a gift to business: like any modern crowd-pleaser, Clara pulled in large audiences who were in a mood to enjoy themselves, buying food and drink as they wandered among the stalls. Furthermore, her presence lent a certain credence to all manner of other wonders and apparently exotic attractions. Contemporary reports reveal a world of unscrupulous showmen attempting to pass off bad actors in even worse costumes as the freakish offspring of unlikely couplings, and inevitably there are also instances of a crowd demanding their money back when a wild man or supposed hybrid species turned out to be particularly lame.

What is particularly striking about the Leipzig fair is the social mix attracted there by Clara. A popular poet, Christian Fürchtegott Gellert, must have queued to see Clara, for he wrote a poem arising from the experience (probably the first original poem about the rhinoceros in European literature). Rubbing shoulders with Gellert, the classicist Friedrich Gotthilf Freytag thought Latin the only conceivable medium for his pamphlet on the nature of the rhinoceros. Liberally sprinkled with quotations from classical Greek authors, Freytag's text neatly illustrates the range of Clara's appeal. As rural labourers stood and stared in wonder, men such as Gellert and Freytag saw Clara through the lens of their own interests and thought how best they might use the experience of a seeing a rhinoceros to demonstrate their literary and philosophical skills. The dissemination of microscopes and telescopes among gentlemen in the previous century had revealed new worlds on both miniature and cosmic scales, but such sights were limited to those with means, education and leisure time. In the mid-eighteenth century, Clara was a novel sight, but knowledge of and access to her was not limited to a moneyed intelligentsia. Representations of her in anything from cheap woodcuts to expensive sculptures often placed her in settings or alongside figures which suggested alien cultures and landscapes, and so the mere sight of Clara became enough to conjure up new or exotic worlds.

In Leipzig, Clara was publicly weighed and measured, as she would be throughout her life. Such a spectacle may seem to offer little in the way of entertainment, but as Van der Meer always allowed locally unimpeachable figures to verify the extraordinary statistics for themselves, many crowds must have enjoyed the sight of a petty official crawling under Clara with a tape measure. Even though she had only been seen to eat hay, suppose she secretly harboured a liking for the taste of bureaucrat? Suppose she crushed someone with her massive weight? Ordinarily, an admission ticket to see Clara promised nothing more than the sight of her eating and sleeping. But anyone who has returned time and again to the zoo enclosure of a resting animal in the hope of seeing it move has experienced the same urges that drew large crowds to public verifications of

Clara's vital statistics. They were certainly impressive: on 1 May 1747 she was declared to be five feet seven inches high, twelve feet long and twelve feet in circumference. A weigh-in one year later in Stuttgart would show that her height had increased to six feet and, although not yet fully grown, she tipped the scales at 5,000 pounds.

Whilst Clara's weight could have been arrived at through a combination of basic mathematics and a little ingenuity, a man with a notebook in hand and a puzzled expression is not a crowd-pleaser. Whereas a rhinoceros held in strapping and lifted from the ground by pulleys more used to the loading and unloading of the heaviest cargoes has obvious appeal. As the machinery strains, the crowd wonders if the animal might fall, or at least become enraged by losing the very ground from under its feet. Clara does not appear to have once given any cause for concern when weighed in this manner, but even so Van der Meer limited his staging of such events. If it made dramatic sense to ensure that Clara's height, weight and girth had clearly increased from one demonstration to another, it also made commercial sense to ensure that he did not harm the rarest and most lucrative animal to have been displayed in Europe.

As he and Clara left Leipzig in early May 1747, Van der Meer could reflect that, in the space of a year, he had won the favour of Frederick the Great, the Empress Maria Theresa and Augustus III. He had been created a Baron of the Holy Roman Empire and had allowed Clara's image to become the exotic face of Meissen porcelain. (With hind-sight, we can see that the most significant historical achievement of the year was the only one that cannot have been apparent to Van der Meer at the time: through her appearance on Meissen ware, Clara had started to replace Dürer's Lisbon rhinoceros of 1515 as the image of the species in Western art.)

The favour of monarchs and the financial rewards of exhibiting Clara were, however, periodically less enticing than the prospect of a rest in comfortable surroundings. The most common ailments to plague captive rhinoceroses today are foot problems exacerbated by the hard ground in parts of zoo enclosures. Older captive rhinoceroses may exhibit all the symptoms of arthritic joints, and watching such a massive animal as it attempts to move between standing and lying down, it is impossible not to be anxious about its obvious discomfort as it rocks back and forth, unable to trust its own legs to take its weight. By May 1747, Clara had spent a year rumbling from the Dutch Republic through Germany and on to Austria, registering every jolt of the road along the way. It was time for a temporary respite – and Van der Meer had an invitation that provided the perfect solution.

Today, the southern German city of Kassel exhibits the remains of one of the most ambitious landscaping projects to be undertaken in eighteenth-century Europe. As the capital of the Electorate of Hesse-Kassel, the city was home to the ruling Landgraves of Hesse, whose ancestral estate of Weissenstein (later Wilhelmshöhe) was remodelled in the early eighteenth century to proclaim their wealth and taste in the most visible manner. At the top of the hillside of the Karlsberg which rises above Kassel, the Landgraves built a giant octagonal wall that was intended to enclose a reservoir. The water supply was to descend the Karlsberg by means of a series of waterfalls to a new villa, from which radial axes were to channel water into the adjacent land-scaped park, with a main axis taking water five kilometres into Kassel itself. Even for the Landgraves' deep pockets, the project threatened to be ruinously expensive and plans for the new villa were ultimately shelved. The Octagon was, however, completed, as a 200-foot-high rusticated structure surmounted by a thirty-foot-tall copper statue of the mythological strongman, Hercules.

As with many of the period's great estates, a basic prem-ise of the design was that viewers would be familiar enough with Greek and Roman mythology to see the statuary and garden monuments simultaneously as representations of classical myths *and* as witty allusions to contemporary poli-tics. (At Versailles, the self-styled 'Sun King' Louis XIV had taken as his alter ego the classical god of the sun, Apollo, and representations of myths showing the triumph of Apollo over his adversaries dominate lines of sight with-in the formal gardens.) In the eighteenth century, the colossal Hercules would have been read as an embodiment of the absolutism of the Electors of Hesse. Clearly visible from the streets of Kassel, the strongman's club was intended to suggest to all who saw it that opposition to such force was doomed to failure.

The wealth which underwrote such grandiose statements of power could, however, provide immense security to those it favoured, and as he left Leipzig, Van der Meer was fortunate that Clara had attracted the interest of the Landgrave Frederick II of Hesse. The invitation to spend a month in Kassel may have placed both rhinoceros and owner at the disposal of the Landgrave's family, but it freed them from the endless rounds of public display and offered them ideal conditions in which to recuperate.

In addition to owning the hillside of the Karlsberg, the rulers of Hesse held private land in Kassel itself. Today, any visitor to the city can take a stroll in the Karlsaue, a park created between 1700 and 1770 as part of the summer retreat favoured by the Landgrave and his family. Within the park, the visitor will find a single-storey building confusingly referred to in much of the tourist literature as the Orangery Palace. The designation implies that this impressive neo-classical edifice was once a palatial family home within the park, but this is a confusion of the structure's original and later uses. Built between 1703 and 1711, the Orangery is one of the finest surviving examples of its kind in Europe. Its original use was as a hothouse, and it was here, in the summer of 1747, that Clara found a temporary home.

If the ownership of classical statues and a landscaped park were meant to be indicators of an eighteenth-century gentleman's wealth and good taste, the presence of rare botanical specimens within his garden was also a potent status symbol. The cultivation of non-native plants that required year-round heating – a luxury well beyond the means of most citizens – was a public proclamation of apparently limitless funds. In the eighteenth century, orangeries therefore became indispensable features of the great landed estates. They were typically constructed as single-storey buildings, and their original function is instantly recognizable by the profusion of large windows running the length of the whole, both front and back. Inside, they are light and airy, their most elaborate décor often being found in wrought-iron grilles on the floor through which the hot air of a hypercaust (or under-floor) heating system was directed towards the orange and lemon trees above.

Any gardener or fruit-grower who has ever wished that more of his fruit had ripened will understand the reasoning behind the enormous scale of these orangeries: only such large-scale planting could guarantee that the whims of a royal court were met. The offer of the Electoral Orangery to Van der Meer might initially seem a strange choice (in preference to, say, the stables of the court) but the building was ideal: it was sufficiently heated to please citrus plants, it provided an abundance of hot water, and its microclimate allowed Clara to trade her habitual fish oil moisturizer for the naturally humid air around her. Indeed, more accustomed to the cramped confines of her wagon, she would have relished the warmth and light of her new surroundings.

The whole idea had surely occurred to the Landgrave as it was widely known that Clara had a particular fondness for oranges. Though the British navy did not appreciate that citrus fruit kept scurvy at bay until well into the eighteenth century, the Dutch East India Company, in whose ranks Van der Meer had been a ship's captain, was well aware of the health-giving properties of fresh fruit and vegetables. It is quite possible, then, that Clara's predilection for oranges (including their peel) had developed as she stood on board the deck of the *Knabenhoe* on her first voyage from India to Leiden, just as had her fondness for the smell of tobacco. When Van der Meer displayed Clara, the pens rigged for her always included as much hay as she could eat and a large bowl of water. Basic food was never withheld as a bribe to stimulate her interest in front of spectators. But should stimulation be required – for example, at a private viewing by a royal audience – Van der Meer could use oranges and tobacco as 'treats' to bring Clara closer or cause her to walk the length of an enclosure or a room.

The Landgrave of Hesse had doubtless been charmed by Clara's public demonstrations of her liking for the fruit. Furthermore, he must have known that the young

members of the Electoral family would be wonderfully
entertained by the thought of a rhinoceros among the
orange trees, while the gardeners would appreciate the
fertilizing properties of her dung. For Clara and Van der
Meer, the benefit of the arrangement was obvious. From
mid-June to mid-July 1747 they were housed at the
Orangery, and no pictures or artefacts are known from this
period: their privacy from public scrutiny was total and
they enjoyed the best their host could offer. The
Landgrave of Hesse did not, however, keep a rhinoceros in
his orangery out of purely altruistic motives, for Clara
allowed Frederick II to flex his political muscle, much to
the envy of Hesse's neighbouring rulers.

Elements of the landscaping of the castle and gardens of
Weissenstein have already been described: the gigantic
garden folly that is the Octagon, surmounted by an obelisk
crowned with a statue of Hercules; the projected radial
waterworks of which only a cascade was ever completed.
The rulers of Hesse may have found that their schemes
could not all be realized on the scale they desired, but the
gardens of the Weissenstein nevertheless played with the
theme of the mythical labours of Hercules in statues and
water effects – fountains and grottoes – intended to signal
the family's importance. According to Greek myth,
Hercules engaged in twelve labours which included divert-
ing the River Eridanus to cleanse the Augean stables. As
the family's ambitions included an artificially constructed

waterway from the Octagon into Kassel itself, the gardens' allusion to Herculean efforts seemed particularly apposite.

Frederick II inherited his estates' framework of classical allusion when he succeeded to the position of Elector of Hesse, but he also nursed horticultural preferences of his own, having already surrounded his Schloss Bellevue with an Anglo-Chinese garden much favoured by his wife Mary, the daughter of the English King George II. (This was possibly the first Chinese-inspired garden in mainland Europe, and Frederick was at the forefront of a craze for chinoiserie both in and out of doors.) In a sense, then, Clara completed the picture. Her exoticism was already empha-sized in posters and porcelain. She was strange and she was rare, and with her in residence at his Orangery, Frederick had a unique and mobile accessory at his command: a stage prop for his oriental gardening interests, and something gratifyingly *different* in the royal line of sight when it gazed on what was otherwise all too familiar.

But like the Hercules atop the Octagon – simultaneously an aesthetic object and an allusion to the invincible power of the rulers of Hesse – Clara held a dual meaning for those who saw her in Kassel. Frederick may have been interest-ed in any garden accessory that suggested the mysterious East, but his primary concern was the maintenance of his political position. The strength of Hercules had bent all to his will: the power of Hesse now commanded a rhinoceros. In France, Louis XV was desperate for a rhinoceros to add to his menagerie; in Rome, the papal gardens were still lacking one, just as they had ever since the Lisbon rhinoceros had sunk without trace in 1516. There was only one rhinoceros to be found in Europe and now all the crowned heads knew it. If only temporarily, Clara allowed Frederick to enjoy the unaccustomed sense of regal one-upmanship, and all for the price of a few oranges.

CHAPTER 5

If Hannibal Could Do It –
Rafting the Rhine

'I believe that there were various plans for transporting
the elephants; at all events the tradition varies as to how it
was accomplished.'
Livy, *History*, XXI, xxviii

Many classical authors tell the story of how Hannibal
led an army on Rome in 218 BC. Marching from
Spain, then across the Pyrenees, Hannibal and his men
evaded capture by the Roman army in Gaul, then fought
their way across the Alps into Italy. Hannibal's is one of the
greatest military feats in history, yet what has given his
story its longevity is not enduring admiration of his battle
plan but amazement at the fact that the Carthaginian
general made his Alpine crossing with elephants, of which
twenty-one were still alive when he reached Italy.

Van der Meer had only one rhinoceros, but his proposed itinerary from the southern German states into Switzerland would have struck any classically educated observer at the time as a latterday variation on Hannibal's campaign. The wagon that had rolled so reliably across the roads of the Holy Roman Empire had now to traverse the mountain passes giving easiest access to the independent Swiss cantons – and an as yet untapped market for Van der Meer's wares. Of course, nothing compelled Van der Meer to visit one state in preference to another, and many in his position might have opted to forego the Swiss market altogether, but Hannibal's ability to marshal his elephants from Gaul into Italy had proved that difficult terrain was not in itself a barrier to the movement of a large, exotic animal.

Clara's Tour may have induced fatigue in both her and her owner, but the last thing Van der Meer wanted was to induce fatigue of a different kind in the viewing public. Publicity material could be re-written and woodcuts varied; models could be produced in a range of media. But one aspect of Clara's tour was unvarying: the slow yet steady progress of her wagon from town to town. Instinctive showman that he was, Van der Meer seems to have realized that topography could be exploited to provide a new twist to reports of Clara's travels. In crossing France, Hannibal had been forced to construct makeshift rafts to take his elephants through the powerful currents of the Rhône. At the southernmost point of her Swiss journey, Clara would be floated into the Swiss cantons on the even greater Rhine. In the process, she would be commemorated in a series of medals struck in her honour, her silver likeness becoming a choice collector's item for gentlemen across Europe. If Hannibal had taken his elephants across mountains and rivers from France into Italy, Van der Meer would traverse similarly difficult terrain in taking Clara from Germany into Switzerland and would capitalize on the fact that she was now sufficiently well known for a wide variety of people to be interested in her fate. From a marketing point of view, a rhinoceros on the Rhine was irresistible.

That Van der Meer took advantage of the river and, in places, its parallel road network to move between Germany and Switzerland in late 1747 and throughout 1748 is the only conclusion that can be drawn from Clara's known itinerary. In chronological order, she moved from Kassel to Mannheim – where she was visited by the Elector Palatine, Carl Theodor, and the entire Electoral family – then on to Strasbourg, Bern, Zurich, Basel, Schaffhausen and Stuttgart. A map of the Rhine valley and the principal towns of the river basin will indicate that a tour through the cities of Bern, Zurich, Basel and Schaffhausen would be a journey from south to north. Put simply, if Clara's wagon rolled south from Strasbourg on into Switzerland, it would be logical to find reports of her visits to Basel, Zurich and Bern – in that order. The historical record indicates the reverse.

It is true that Van der Meer could have chosen to skirt around Basel and Zurich in order to make Bern Clara's first Swiss stop, but at a time when even the best roads were relatively primitive, there could have been no good reason for risking Clara's wagon off the beaten track to avoid two major cities, only to return to them later. Given Strasbourg's location on the west bank of the Rhine, the obvious solution to the puzzle is that, following her stay in Strasbourg in December 1747, Van der Meer obtained passage for his party on a vessel heading up the Rhine and sailed the river to its navigable conclusion. Clara was then disembarked in Switzerland, from where her wagon rolled overland to Bern, then on to Zurich and Basel.

Following visits to other German cities, Van der Meer would return in November 1748 to Leiden, where it is known that Clara was drawn and sculpted by the anatomist Petrus Camper. Yet once one appreciates how Van der Meer could have used both ordinary freight vessels and extraordinary timber transporters to his advantage in moving up and down the Rhine, it is clear that, for an eighteenth-century audience, the details of this stage of Clara's Tour would have emulated some of the most dramatic elements of Hannibal's story. Yet whilst the death of a single elephant would not have damaged Hannibal's military campaign, Van der Meer possessed the only rhinoceros in all of Europe: Clara simply could not be lost. As it was, the very nature of her fame was about to be transformed, for Clara would soon become the unwitting originator of that most modern media equation: if you place a celebrity in an unfamiliar and possibly dangerous situation, public interest will increase dramatically – and so will your financial rewards.

Clara's visit to Strasbourg in December 1747 marked the beginning of a new phase in her marketing. Here the Kamm family, metalworkers of distinction, struck three separate designs of medals celebrating the presence of a rhinoceros in the city. Commemorative medals have a history almost as old as coinage itself and have long attracted the attention of specialist collectors. In the eighteenth century, however, commemorative medals with limited production runs attracted the interest of not only dedicated numismatists but also every gentleman with a cabinet of curiosities to maintain. The British Minister in Florence, Sir Horace Mann, whose correspondence made mention of Van der Meer's ennoblement, told his friend Sir Horace Walpole that, whilst the Roman Emperor Augustus proudly displayed a rhinoceros in the arena, 'I have never heard that a medal of it was struck, as has now been done in honour of this, one of which has been sent to me from Rome, and, which, if it was worthwhile, I would send you to enrich your cabinet' (letter dated Florence, 13 March 1750).

Though Mann's comments suggest that a medal of Clara struck in Italy in 1750 would not be an especially fine addition to Walpole's collection, the first medals of Clara, struck in Strasbourg, clearly initiated a vogue for recording her visits in a durable form. Less fragile than porcelain or canvas and considerably more portable than marble, medals of bronze and silver disseminated knowledge of Clara among gentlemen collectors across Europe. As her likeness was cast, so the medal inscriptions from Strasbourg provide verification of Clara's weight in 1747: speculation about what a rhinoceros looked like was replaced with an enduring record. And the animal that generated so much money itself became a token in circulation, as sought after by those with display cabinets as Clara was sought after for public display.

After Strasbourg, Van der Meer aimed at the Swiss cantons. Outside the territory of the Holy Roman Empire, the major Swiss cities and their hinterland enjoyed an admired history of political and religious independence, favouring republican government and, in places, an uncompromising Calvinism. For many eighteenth-century British and French writers, Switzerland was synonymous with freedom. (Voltaire would maintain a chateau in the French town of Ferney and a town house just across the Swiss border in the city of Geneva that might serve as a convenient bolt-hole at times of difficulty with the French authorities.)

Travelling from Germany into Switzerland was not easy, but the border controls that many Grand Tourists found annoying, and sometimes even threatening, were not to be the cause of Van der Meer's problems at this stage of the journey. He enjoyed the favour of local dignitaries wherever he travelled with Clara, and so one presumes that Maria Theresa's imperial approval had been translated into letters of transit allowing him considerable freedom of movement throughout the Holy Roman Empire. And besides, any border guard who was suspicious of the Dutchman and his heavy wagon had only to look inside to be assured that this was not a situation encompassed by the usual paperwork.

Rather, Van der Meer's problems were of a more basic kind: he simply dare not risk Clara's wagon on the roads running parallel to the Rhine. One of the most detailed eighteenth-century accounts of an attempted crossing from Germany into Switzerland via the coaching routes of the Rhine valley has been left by the English Gothic horror novelist, Ann Radcliffe, whose travels through southern Germany in 1794 afforded her only a glimpse of the Swiss mountains before she was forced to turn back by a combination of intransigent border guards and poor coaching facilities. 'Throughout Germany,' Radcliffe wrote, 'you will not meet more than one [carriage] in twenty miles. Travelling is considered by the natives, who know the fatigue of going in carriages nearly without springs, and stopping at inns where there is little of either accommodation or civility, as productive of no pleasure.' The roads of the southern Rhine valley only multiplied the difficulties identified by Radcliffe: they tended to be very narrow, and there was often the danger of debris falling from overhangs. This was not terrain in which to risk an eight-strong horse team and a wagon of unusual size and weight. But why travel by road when Strasbourg provided the opportunity to embark upon one of Europe's greatest waterways?

Along the course of the Rhine, river barges plied their trade, transporting goods between some of the major cities of the Holy Roman Empire: upriver from Strasbourg, the Rhine was navigable into Switzerland (albeit with a delay for disembarkation and reloading at the Rhine Falls near Schaffhausen); downriver, the Rhine would lead to the Dutch Republic and ultimately to the North Sea. Van der Meer had simply to find a barge owner who had spare capacity on deck and was willing to grant passage to a rhinoceros, and two things guaranteed Van der Meer a favourable hearing: a large amount of ready money and his Dutch nationality. As Ann Radcliffe told her readers later in the century, the Dutch were the most distinctive group of Rhine bargemen, possessed of the best transports: 'We could not find more than thirty vessels of burthen against the quay, all mean and ill-built, except the Dutch, which are very large, and . . . constructed purposely for a tedious navigation.'

The diaries of a range of eighteenth-century Grand Tourists indicate that their favoured mode of transport was a light-bodied carriage which was capable of being dismantled for transportation by barge or over the Alps. Casanova's

memoirs detail the ingenuity of one of his manservants in
rigging sailcloth around the dismembered body of a coach,
in order that the Count and his current mistress could enjoy
themselves privately on deck, cocooned by their surrounding possessions as their barge floated through the night
towards Venice. By contrast, Clara's wagon was neither
light nor made to be dismantled, but its hoisting aboard
and transportation would not have presented great difficulties to a bargeman used to heavy cargoes. As for Clara, she
had already proved that she was a good sailor – compliant
on deck when familiar with those around her and given
large quantities of food.

It is unlikely that Van der Meer negotiated passage for
the team of eight horses needed to pull the wagon: coaching inns allowed the moneyed tourist the opportunity to
hire fresh horses for the next stage of a journey, while
obtaining and disposing of horse teams at will would have
been easy for a man enjoying the status that Clara had
brought her owner by late 1747. Whether, at this stage, anyone else was permanently retained by Van der Meer to
accompany them on their travels is not recorded, but it is
probable he employed at least one male assistant with
whom Clara was familiar. Such hired help would not have
been necessary to control Clara: she may have been
hostage to Van der Meer's quest for fame and fortune but,
knowing no other life than that of the road and being
reliant on Van der Meer to feed her gargantuan appetite,

Clara was most unlikely to make a bid for freedom if left unguarded. Van der Meer and any assistant could sleep soundly at night, for this was when Clara also slept. Van der Meer would none the less have appreciated an additional pair of trusty hands – and eyes – whenever errands had to be run and an unguarded Clara would otherwise be at the mercy of the curious. Indeed, any ambitious young man with an interest in travel and possessing reasonable German and French would surely have welcomed the opportunity to remain part of Clara's entourage under Van der Meer's watchful direction and experience its periodic brushes with aristocratic society.

For Clara, the voyage upstream would have been as pleasurable as her time spent in the Orangery at Kassel: the confines of her wagon had once again been exchanged for air and light, there was no longer the bone-shaking jolt of the road, and Van der Meer and his assistant would be attending to her every need. Horse teams were still a feature of her journey, but now they were drawing the barge upstream against even the strongest currents. The sight of a rhinoceros and her heavy-bodied wagon on board a barge must have been an extraordinary one for other river traffic or viewers from the bank, and none of this would have been lost on Van der Meer. For Clara was going to make further journeys by water, and her ever-enterprising owner would exploit the inherent drama – and potential danger – of transporting her in this way, and with very lucrative results.

No matter the astonishment they inspired on the river or on shore, for Clara and Van der Meer this journey was uneventful. The barge on which they had gained passage in Strasbourg would have been forced to unload just outside Schaffhausen, where all Rhine traffic stopped and passengers and cargoes were briefly transferred overland in order to avoid the nearby falls. Clara could easily have walked this stage of the journey, though the temptation to graze must have been irresistible and only the allure of oranges or tobacco might have persuaded her to move on. At no stage could Van der Meer have forced Clara to do anything against her wishes: the thick skin of the Indian rhinoceros will not register an admonitory tap from a human hand, whilst the use of any implement to deliver a reprimand that a rhinoceros might feel would only provoke it to anger. Clara could not be physically led: she had never had a ring fixed through her nose, and so she would stop and eat whenever she pleased – unless, of course, the smell of something more interesting than grass caught her attention. Van der Meer had surely taken the opportunity afforded by the Landgrave's hospitality at Kassel to stock all available space in and on the wagon with produce from the Orangery. But manoeuvring a rhinoceros around a waterfall armed with nothing more than a tempting basket of fruit was, like every other aspect of Clara's journey, an achievement borne of necessity and inspiration in equal measure. Like Hannibal before him, Van der Meer improvised as he went along.

Upriver from the Rhine Falls, the journey resumed into Switzerland. Taking the Rhine almost to the limits of its upper navigable extent, the party disembarked and obtained the necessary horse team. (Wherever the bargemen plied their trade, fresh horse teams were available for hire to pull the vessels against the current.) The city of Bern is the site of Clara's first known public appearance in Switzerland, and any relief map of the area will readily suggest that Van der Meer must have taken her wagon overland from their Rhine disembarkation, following the best route suggested by the surrounding topography to Bern.

On 27 January 1748, Clara was available for public viewings in the city but, unusually, Van der Meer relinquished control of an important element her display. For the first time on Clara's Tour, the price of public admission was determined not by Van der Meer or by viewers themselves, but by two local councillors. The implications of this are worth pausing over, for in Clara Van der Meer as good as controlled a monopoly and he did not need to cultivate the favour of the town council, either in Bern or anywhere else: we may assume, therefore, that he saw some benefit in the involvement of local officials in his business. But what was an appropriate sum to pay to see the only rhinoceros in the Western world? When the question is posed in these terms, it already suggests its own answer: the councillors thought

Van der Meer justified in charging a premium whilst the Dutchman let it be known that the council itself had approved the charge made for Clara's display. For those sober citizens rarely tempted by the dubious attractions of travelling fairs, the knowledge that their local representatives had determined the entrance fee was reassuring and suggested that here was something worth seeing. However the arrangement came about, it guaranteed excellent publicity.

For the town councils of Zurich and Basel, it must have seemed that the governors of Bern had established a useful precedent for dealing with the travelling Dutchman: as Van der Meer negotiated the Swiss tour beyond Bern, he again met the demand that officials be allowed to determine entry fees to see Clara. As they were in effect licensing the display of Clara, it is inconceivable that the Swiss town councils did not demand a share of the profits she realized. And since Van der Meer was content to agree to such terms throughout the Swiss cantons, he must have been making good enough money to feel able to surrender that share.

Woodcuts produced for her visit to Zurich in March 1748 indicate that councillors appear to have decided upon a sliding scale of charges (eight, four or two baçes) according to income and how closely Clara was viewed. It is possible to convert eighteenth-century Swiss currency into modern amounts, but not especially revealing. Rather, what the variation in charges seems to illustrate is that there was *no* typical viewer, some citizens paying up to four times as much as others. Here was a visitor attraction that was truly classless and that all classes wished to see.

Souvenirs of the experience were likewise available to all, but the difference between the highest- and lowest-priced of these items is noticeably greater than that between the highest- and lowest-priced entrance tickets. Two groschen would buy a poster illustrated with a woodcut – primitive, but with text nevertheless specific to this stage of the tour in 1748. For two baçes, the eager viewer could acquire a small copper engraving of Clara showing sharper definition than the woodcut and more suitable for hanging on a wall. The viewer with four baçes to spare could buy a larger copper engraving, accompanied by text in French, German, Dutch and Latin, the latter still *the* language of learning in mid-eighteenth-century Europe.

Marketing ploys were not, however, confined to posters or engravings. For the princely sum of twelve baçes, a medal commemorating Clara's visit could be purchased, suggesting that such artefacts were bought by gentlemen to be shown to their friends, perhaps along with other numismatic treasures and exotic insect life, all displayed in cabinets of curiosities. Although the Kamm family of Strasbourg are Clara's only medal casters to be known by name, it is likely that Van der Meer employed local metal workers wherever Clara travelled in the upper Rhine valley.

Van der Meer could have stocked up on medals produced by the Kamms in December 1747, and thereby
saved himself both the time Clara spent sitting for new
castings and their relatively small costs. But Clara was to
visit some of the most famous metal-working centres of
Switzerland and Germany, and in commissioning new
medals from local craftsmen at every stage of this part of
the tour, Van der Meer guaranteed the immediate professional interest – and personal curiosity – of the powerful
and influential guilds. As he immortalized Clara's Tour in a
series of commemorative medals, Van der Meer in the
process turned Clara's image into a highly desirable collector's item. Medals had since classical times celebrated great
achievements and triumphal moments; from 1747 onwards,
they would celebrate an equally historical event – the visit
to a town of Europe's only rhinoceros.

From Zurich, Clara travelled north-west to Basel, Van
der Meer being careful to keep the heavy wagon away from
the worst mountain roads. Since a stay in Schaffhausen is
recorded in the second half of March, where official paperwork details the ruling council's determination of entrance
fees after the manner of Zurich and Basel, it is quite possible that Van der Meer negotiated passage on a Rhine barge
a second time, for the leg of the journey from Basel to
Schaffhausen. A topographical map of the region will show
that the easiest way from one town to another is a journey
on the river that flows between them, and anything that

took the pressure off the wheels of Clara's wagon must have been welcomed.

From Schaffhausen, a cross-country route was planned, taking Clara through the Black Forest to Stuttgart. It is tempting to imagine Clara being liberated from the confines of her wagon as Van der Meer and his assistant slowly made their way north: even more tempting to picture the incredulity on the faces of the local peasantry as a rhinoceros and two men passed by with no more explanation than a foreign-sounding 'Good morning'. But this is merely wishful thinking. Since a rhinoceros maps the world around it largely through its sense of smell, human planning can do little to make the stony road ahead more attractive than the distracting smells of the forest. We know Clara responded to bribery in the form of oranges, but Van der Meer's stock of fruit must have been nearly exhausted, and besides, too much citric acid will impact on even the most robust of digestive systems. So Clara is unlikely to have shocked any Black Forest woodcutters by walking through their clearings. Only when the horse team needed rest and the wagon became the centre of an impromptu camp at night would she have been able to explore the unfamiliar and tantalizing smells around her.

Clara's visit to Stuttgart in May 1748 was the occasion of a very public weigh-in. It is therefore possible to record that, on 6 May 1748, she was a healthy 5,000 pounds. In the twenty-first century, we can readily conceive of Clara's

weight in relation to that of, say, a car. A mid-eighteenth-
century audience had no such point of comparison. Clara
was bigger, heavier and stranger than anything in their
wildest imaginings. The notion that there were places
where such creatures were not uncommon must have
seemed incredible.

Against this background, the decision to celebrate the
visit of such an animal with a commemorative medal
becomes more understandable, and Stuttgart yielded one
of five different medal designs known from this stage of
Clara's tour. From Stuttgart the party headed south-east
and is next recorded in Augsburg from mid-May to mid-
June of 1748. But it is apparent from any map of the area
that, approximately two-thirds of the way from Stuttgart to
Augsburg, all roads – and the River Danube – go through
the city of Ulm. It would be strange if Van der Meer
had bypassed such a thriving commercial and intellectual
centre under any circumstances, but it seems especially
unlikely given the area's historic association with large,
exotic animals.

Boasting the tallest church tower in the world (at over
four hundred feet), Ulm Cathedral was begun in 1376 and
only eventually completed some five centuries later. The
cathedral has many points of interest, and so it would be
easy to overlook the stained-glass window that interprets
the creation story of Genesis and features an elephant
coming forth from the hand of its creator, harnessed and

armoured for battle: a distinct martial oddity in the Garden of Eden. But this is not the only pachyderm to be found in the region: in the forecourt of the Castle of Wiesensteig, the fountain pours from a sixteenth-century stone elephant. These and other representations of the animal in the region may be traced to claims made by the local Counts of Helfenstein to be descended from a Roman citizen who was actively engaged in the defeat of Hannibal and his elephant army. (Thus the armoured elephant in the stained glass of Ulm Cathedral says less about a Christian vision of creation than it does about the potency of a local legend.)

Few of those who saw Clara at this time would have been able to read the Roman historian Livy, but many must have heard versions of the writer's account of Hannibal's expedition, related by one generation to another as a way of accounting for the representations of the strange creatures to be found across the nearby countryside. For Van der Meer, the popular currency of Hannibal's story may well have determined his immediate plans. The known itinerary of the tour following Augsburg is a trek north to Nuremberg, the sixteenth-century home of Dürer, which occupied the party until late August 1748. Documentary evidence then indicates a journey north-west to Würzburg where, on 3 October 1748, the painter Anton Lünenscholoss explained the subject of a drawing with the inscription 'called Miss Clara' ('*wird genannt die Jungfer Clara*'). As 'Miss Clara' is then recorded as having returned home to Leiden, in time to be modelled by a second anatomist, Petrus Camper, in December 1748, something unusual clearly happened. One moment, Clara was enjoying the collective affections of the citizens of Würzburg in the southern half of modern-day Germany. The next time she can be placed, it is many hundreds of miles away on the Dutch coast.

As with her journey into the Swiss cantons, a map both highlights the problem and immediately suggests the solution. Having picked up passage on a Rhine barge to take them into Switzerland, Van der Meer must have been content to make use of the river again as Würzburg gives easy access to routes west to both Mannheim and Wiesbaden on the Rhine. Taking passage downriver, there was no need to employ a steady Dutch barge, pulled by horses against the flow of the water. And among all the craft plying their trade on the river, the most astonishing were not permanent vessels at all, but huge agglomerations of timber, floating with the current towards dispersal and sale in the Dutch Republic. Crewed by men who made their temporary homes on the timbers, the giant rafts may have convinced Van der Meer that, not for the first time on this stage of Clara's tour, Hannibal was worth emulating, and to spectacular effect.

Even before Hannibal contemplated the logistics of moving a small herd of elephants across the Alps, he had to find a means of transporting the nervous animals across the swiftly flowing Rhône. Since the crossing of a river seems less noteworthy than hazarding the Alps, the details of this early part of Hannibal's campaign are perhaps less well known, yet Livy makes them as compelling as the more celebrated feat. Realizing that his elephants would not venture into the water of their own accord, Hannibal lured them onto substantial wooden rafts that had been lashed together. As the animals were driven from one raft to another, Hannibal's men worked in the river around them, moving the raft just vacated nearest to the bank out into the middle of the current, so constructing a floating, moving bridge to the furthest side of the water.

Doubts regarding the veracity of Livy's text are understandable: how many mature trees does a travelling army need to fell before it can build a raft capable of accommodating one or more elephants? For generations of readers, worries about such practicalities have finally been subsumed in the knowledge that, however unlikely it seems, Hannibal did achieve his immediate aim of moving the large, frightened animals across first a substantial river and then one of Europe's most formidable mountain ranges. But Van der Meer did not need to worry about providing himself with a makeshift raft to take Clara down the Rhine. In the eighteenth century, Rhine rafts came ready-made.

The Gothic novelist Ann Radcliffe has also left a vivid account of what she saw when visiting Germany and the Netherlands in 1795, and much of what she witnessed could have been seen earlier in the century. Her account of the 'timber floats' on the Rhine testifies to both her amazement and determination to understand what she was seeing:

> The length is from seven hundred to one thousand feet; the breadth from fifty to ninety; the depth, when manned with the whole crew, usually seven feet. The trees in the principal rafts are not less than seventy feet long, of which ten compose a raft. On this sort of floating island, five hundred labourers of different classes are employed, maintained and lodged, during the whole voyage; and a little street of deal huts is built upon it for their reception.

Detailing the layers of timber laid crosswise on top of each other to give solidity to the whole, Radcliffe explains that 'the surface is rendered even; storehouses and other apartments are raised: and the whole is again strengthened by large masts of oak'. The men on board worked hard and the merchants who hoped to profit from the final sale of the timber rewarded them accordingly. Though they slept on straw, eighty to one hundred men at a time, all were well fed: 'The consumption of provisions on board such a float is estimated for each voyage at fifteen or twenty thousand pounds of fresh meat, between forty and fifty thousand pounds of bread . . . and five or six hundred tons of beer.' Transporting, entirely incidentally, an abundance of straw, bread and beer – the staples of Clara's diet – to be enjoyed all the way north, the enormous rafts offered rough and ready facilities to anyone able to secure themselves a passage.

As a former sea captain, Van der Meer was used to worse conditions than those on the rafts and he could offer ready payment both for his and his assistant's transport and for Clara's daily provisions. The crews of the rafts were men whose working lives involved regularly risking mutilation or worse as they lashed the timbers together in the churning current, and so they were unlikely to mutiny when confronted with a tame rhinoceros, especially one eager to follow the smell of a bowl of beer. And so it is entirely possible that, standing on the banks of the Rhine in late 1748, watching the familiar timber rafts drift past, a viewer might have suddenly stopped and stared as the elephant's nemesis, the rhinoceros, went floating down the river. To anyone familiar with the Helfensteins' legendary association with Hannibal, history was being re-enacted with a most novel twist.

For Van der Meer, a river journey back to Leiden offered the chance to rest both Clara and the wheels of her carriage. Once embarked upon their journey northwards, the Rhine timber rafts rarely docked in towns along the way, and so the spoils of three years' worth of travel could therefore be safely housed on part of the massive deck. And if any crewmen were tempted by the Dutchman's money bags, the raft was conspicuously lacking in places for hiding stolen goods.

If Van der Meer had any pressing financial concerns, they probably related not to the trustworthiness of the raft's crew, but to the stability of Europe's financial markets. Of necessity, most of the money earned through Clara's display must have been converted into bills and bonds that would be transformed back into the solid reassurance of gold and silver by the Dutch representatives of Europe's rudimentary banking network. Yet the money had never been simply the product of ticket sales: from the moment when Wandelaar engraved Clara for the anatomist Albinus, Van der Meer understood that a range of professionals would pay him for the chance to use Clara's image to promote their own work. If anything, the routine display of Clara was less lucrative than an agreement that her likeness should be reproduced on canvas or in porcelain – something of which Van der Meer had been reminded even before he embarked on the journey north.

In Augsburg, agreement had been reached that Clara should be sketched by Johann Elias Ridinger, with a view to the production of a series of engravings. Six of Ridinger's studies of Clara are known today, all executed in June 1748. Since Ridinger had a dedicated following among the European nobility for his more usual animal subjects and hunting scenes, his satisfaction can be imagined at finding something both original and fashionable to offer to his wealthy patrons. Of all his studies of Clara, the most charming is a sketch, *The Dutch Rhinoceros Lying on its Left Side* (now in the Courtauld Institute, London). Clara stretches out in front of us, her front legs slightly bent under her, and her head extended on the ground. The great folds of skin of the neck are observed in detail, as is the texture of the skin: Ridinger draws tightly packed tubercles on the right front leg and body, as though he wants at least one area of the sketch to remind him of the unique qualities of the Indian rhinoceros's hide. So closely observed is this drawing that it is impossible to imagine Ridinger executing it from more than a few feet away from a sleeping Clara. Given that her acute sense of smell would alert her to the presence of a stranger, even in her sleep, the intimacy of the drawing suggests Clara's total ease in human company.

Ridinger appears to have kept – and then sold – all of what he produced as a result of these sketching sessions. Clearly, it is implausible that Van der Meer paid Ridinger to draw Clara and then declined to take any examples of the work he had commissioned: Ridinger must therefore have paid Van der Meer for a day's access to Clara, the two men agreeing that the artist would retain ownership of all the drawings (and later engravings) made.

Van der Meer surely realized that, as more images of Clara appeared in circulation, Clara's worth did not diminish but rather increased. Only such a confidence in the appetite of the market can have prompted his own commissioning of a silver medal from Gözinger of Ansbach, as well as five different medal designs from Werner of Nuremberg. And it is a fitting coincidence that the home city of Dürer, in which he produced his influential *Rhinoceros* of 1515, should have become one of the sites from which a host of correctives to that image would be produced.

The drawings, engravings and medals produced for Clara's Rhineland tour of 1747–8 were still not enough to satisfy the curiosity of some regarding the appearance of the rhinoceros. Arriving home in Leiden towards the end of 1748, Van der Meer received a very different request to any previously made in respect of Clara. Whereas Albinus had wished to include Clara in the anatomical plates engraved for him by Wandelaar, the young anatomist who now presented himself to Van der Meer had no particular interest in a mutually beneficial publishing venture. Petrus Camper was both an anatomist and artist, his primary focus being the relatively new field of comparative anatomy. Making accurate scale drawings of all species he could see, Camper was, without realizing it, already amassing the raw material that he would synthesize in his later works, where the meticulous outlines of a variety of quadrupeds are superimposed upon each other and around a series of axes. In showing the arc through which a horse's neck is capable of moving, and superimposing this upon the outline and limits of movement of a heavier creature, Camper attempts to show his readers why the animal kingdom looks and moves in the way that it does. (Just over a hundred years later, in 1859, Charles Darwin would publish a more famous account of these and related ideas in *The Origin of Species*.)

According to Camper, the qualities of extreme agility, great height and massive weight cannot occur in the same species, for nature can only manifest itself in certain ways: the unicorn cannot exist, not because no one has ever seen one, but because no land species has a cranial structure capable of supporting the weight of a single mass of bone above the eyes. (Even in water, such a weight cannot be supported: the male narwhal's single tusk is technically a tooth growing from the parts of the mouth.) In undertaking research for a work that would finally be entitled *On the Absurdity of the Supposed Unicorns* (1787), Camper wished to see as many horned animals as possible. The final version of the text shows his knowledge of species of antelope, elephant, Ethiopian pig, ox, ram, stag reindeer, walrus – and rhinoceros.

Camper's letters and surviving works show that a meeting with Clara was clearly arranged in the winter of 1748, when he drew her and modelled her in clay. This was, however, no ordinary modelling session. When Camper finally went to press to declare the absurdity of any residual belief in unicorns, he acknowledged that his readers were probably aware of the Indian rhinoceros whose skull supports a single horn, in apparent contradiction to his assertion that no land animal could sustain such an additional weight of bone on the skull, and in such proximity to the vertebrae of the neck. Camper is sure his readers will know that the horn of the Indian rhinoceros stands 'on the nasal bones', but they can be forgiven for falling into the common error of assuming that rhinoceros horn is made of bone.

The best description Camper can find for the horn of the Indian rhinoceros is that it is like the 'hardened bodies' that protrude from the head of the giraffe. His description suggests a man who has examined both an Indian rhinoceros and a giraffe at close quarters, touching the nasal horn, registering its difference to ivory and bone. Modern science confirms his observation: all species of rhinoceros alive today have a horn composed of keratin, the building block of human hair and nails. What appears at first sight to be a variant on antlers and tusks bears no physical resemblance to them at all. And since the horn is composed of keratin, it does not require the massive structural support that would be needed were it composed of bone. On a mature rhinoceros, the horn grows from a spongy mass of tissue: if lost, or shed, it will grow again, much as do the human nails to which it is so closely related.

Camper's time with Clara in late 1748 was not, then, a conventional studio session with artist and model. If Clara had allowed Ridinger to approach within a few feet to sketch her, she now allowed Camper to examine her horn at close quarters. Just as the proliferation of her image in a range of media across Europe suggested the limitations of Dürer's archetype, so her centrality to Camper's work suggested the improbability of ever finding a unicorn. Indeed, once Clara had been seen in the flesh, it became abundantly clear that both Dürer's *Rhinoceros* and the mythical unicorn were false representations of the natural world: neither animal could possibly possess the horn with which it had been credited.

By now Van der Meer had travelled throughout the Holy Roman Empire and the Swiss cantons and floated down the Rhine with a rhinoceros, so it is unlikely that he was surprised by much: if others wished to have time with Clara in order to disprove the existence of unicorns, if Clara seemed content that Camper should examine all round her horn, and if enough money were paid, the arrangement was satisfactory enough. When Camper subsequently engaged in a very public dispute with Albinus, calling into question the latter's accuracy in his famous anatomical atlas, it may have struck Van der Meer as surprising that two of the most famous and talented anatomists in Leiden, united in their interest in Clara, could descend into slanderous dispute about each other's general competence. In Clara, Van der Meer had a catalyst for endless debate, but he himself had little time for, or interest in, the details of others' arguments. The end of the year was fast approaching, and Clara and Van der Meer were shortly expected at Versailles.

CHAPTER 6

All Things to All Men –
Rhinomania at Versailles

'All Paris, so easily inebriated by small objects, is now busy
with a kind of animal called rhinoceros.'
Grimm to Diderot, 1749

In 1956, the Spanish surrealist artist Salvador Dali
addressed a crowd at the Palais des Expositions in Paris.
The more conventional of his two stage props was a bust
of the great eighteenth-century French satirist, Voltaire.
The other, swaying precariously above the bust and
suspended by a crane, was a large model rhinoceros. In an
unpredictable moment of stagecraft, the rhinoceros was
lowered onto the bust of Voltaire, crushing it and releasing a deluge of milk from one or possibly both of the
props.

In his later years, Dali had become obsessed with

135

rhinoceros horns, and batteries of them appear in his paintings. History does not record whether he knew of Voltaire's genuine interest in the rhinoceros, but the Surrealist's treatment of the philosopher's bust may still serve as a fitting symbol for the tide of rhinomania that was about to sweep Paris in 1749. Where *philosophes* such as Voltaire were concerned to understand the nature of the beast, the city's fashionable world was about to go wild for all things rhinocerotic. Thus, while anatomical and evolutionary knowledge derived from Clara was incorporated into two of the most ambitious publishing projects of the eighteenth century, Diderot and d'Alembert's twenty-eight-volume *Encyclopédie* (1751–72) and Buffon's forty-four-volume *Histoire Naturelle* (1749–1804), Parisian society pondered what struck it as equally weighty questions, such as how hair, clothes and carriage horses might be accessorized *à la rhinocéros*. In a Paris accustomed to being in thrall to the preferences of the King's current mistress, Clara was about to find herself at the centre of both the social and the scientific whirl.

Reports indicate that Clara's wagon rolled through Rheims at the very end of 1748, *en route* to the French court at Versailles. The preferred residence of Louis XIV and a magnet for some ten thousand courtiers and nobles at any one time, Versailles offered the French monarchy a self-contained retreat from its capital, two hours' carriage ride away. Indeed, Louis XIV had found his life so comfortable at the chateau that, by the time he died in 1715, he had managed to survive both the son and grandson next in line to the throne. When Louis XV succeeded his great-grand-father, his inheritance included the Sun King's two menageries: one at Vincennes to the east of Paris and one at Versailles to the west.

Under Louis XIV, the stock of the royal menageries had been used to demonstrate absolute royal power: in 1682, for example, the Persian ambassador had found a combat between a tiger and elephant being staged in his honour. Determined to show that he had prize specimens to spare, Louis XIV even insisted that the animals be made to fight to the death. But Louis XV did not care for something so reminiscent of the Roman games: indeed, as Clara approached Versailles in January 1749, uncomfortable questions were being asked in radical quarters about the value of the royal menageries. The justification that such places were instructive – of benefit to natural historians and those interested in comparative anatomy – was already being countered by doubts that the lions at Versailles gave any real indication of how these animals behaved in the wild. (Such doubts have a surprisingly contemporary ring to them, for now we identify so-called 'repetitive' modes of behaviour in zoo animals – the pacing of cages, say, or the repeated movement of the head through particular arcs – and associate them with stress.)

Nevertheless, at the outset of Louis XV's reign, between

forty and fifty carriages a day, each capable of holding up to four people, made the journey from Paris to Versailles, where the menagerie was open to the public. Approached via a gallery which led into an octagonal viewing chamber, the seven radial enclosures of the menagerie were visible from viewing balconies outside each of the chamber's walls. An early example of the panopticon that Jeremy Bentham would later propose as the best design for penal institutions, the menagerie allowed a centrally placed viewer to contemplate the power of a king of France whose colonial territories yielded such diverse and exotic species.

Whilst Louis XIV had understood and cultivated the symbolic power of the menagerie, Louis XV preferred to cultivate the company of his mistress, Madame de Pompadour, his botanical specimens and the royal collection of poultry. At the time of Clara's visit, the most exotic animals already in residence at Versailles included a camel, two lions, two tigers, a pelican and a seal. To some of the king's ministers, the neglect of the menagerie seemed politically inadvisable, for reasons neatly summarized in a printed guide of 1755: 'It could be said that Africa has paid a tribute of her productions, and that other parts of the world have given as homage to the king their most rare and unusual animals and birds.' Ensuring an influx of new species into the menagerie was politically expedient, for it signalled France's imperial reach: an Indian rhinoceros in the menagerie might suggest that all was well with France's

Indian territories (though these would eventually be ceded to France's imperial rival, Britain, by the Treaty of Paris of 1763).

But Louis XV was more interested in hunting and had, between 1735 and 1739, commissioned eight huge canvases on the theme of *Chasses exotiques*, depicting men in pursuit of a range of wild animals including an elephant, a leopard and a crocodile. So his interest in Clara may well have been stimulated by the chance to see the fabled enemy of the elephant in the flesh. Whatever prompted the invitation to Van der Meer to house Clara at Versailles throughout January 1749, the king's ministers could congratulate themselves on this public relations coup. Even critics of the royal menageries would find the chance to see a rhinoceros irresistible and, as a result, the value of the collections would be less open to question. Not for the first time, Clara's tour was used by others to further their own social and political agendas.

What happened next at Versailles proved impossible to keep out of the public domain. At some time during January, doubtless in response to the King's evident fascination with Clara, Van der Meer offered to sell her to Louis for 100,000 écus – a sum that in 1749 would have kept a prince of the blood in truly regal style for a good three years. Though he had probably never expressed such a sentiment in his life, Louis XV now found himself in the position of declaring an asking price to be too high. Worse

still for Van der Meer, the King was insulted by the audac-
ity of a financial demand that amounted to years of royal
expenditure.

What possessed the usually astute Dutchman to ask for
such a sum? The possibility that Louis expressed the wish
to acquire Clara and that Van der Meer, unwilling to part
with her, deliberately priced her beyond even the King's
reach is attractive but unlikely. Louis would in due course
bankroll the construction and furnishing of the Petit
Trianon and Hermitage at Versailles for Madame de
Pompadour: he could always command funds if the expenditure seemed to him sufficiently important. So money was
not the problem, although Van der Meer was hardly in any
position to predict on what Louis might choose to spend it.
Furthermore, to engineer a deliberate deal-breaker with
one of the most powerful and absolutist monarchies in
Europe would have been foolhardy in the extreme, and
Van der Meer was nothing if not a pragmatist. He genuinely
seems to have believed that Louis XV would find 100,000
écus an acceptable asking price for the only rhinoceros then
on European soil.

One can see how Louis XV might have viewed the transaction. When an Indian rhinoceros was finally installed in
the Versailles menagerie on 11 September 1770, it was a
gift to the king from Chevalier, the governor of an isolated
French enclave in what was rapidly becoming British India.
(It was the same rhinoceros whose transportation from the

port of Lorient to Versailles so exercised the wheelwrights charged with constructing its transportation.) This was fitting, for Louis had been brought up to believe in his privilege in all things and he apparently expected that permanent exhibits would be given rather than sold to the royal menageries. As a Dutchman and a citizen of a great mercantile nation, Van der Meer expected appropriate recompense for parting with his livelihood. The King and the sea captain therefore opened their negotiations from very different positions.

Given all that Clara had achieved for Van der Meer, his willingness to part with her may seem to be evidence of a cold and utilitarian character. This is a possibility, of course, but one can venture a more charitable interpretation. Van der Meer had already spent long periods on the road with Clara and her display had brought him wealth and fame. But were he to cease her exhibition, Clara's appetite would quickly begin to erode Van der Meer's savings. Furthermore, believing as he did that she might live for a hundred years, the Dutchman simply could not retire Clara so soon – not least because there was no eighteenth-century equivalent of the RSPCA that might have taken her from Van der Meer and provided her with a comfortable life in retirement, away from the public gaze. (Quite the reverse – when an Indian rhinoceros presented to Philip II of Spain in 1581 became a problem for its captors, the preferred solution had been the blinding of the unfortunate animal and the removal of its horn.)

In short, having brought Clara from India for the express purpose of displaying her across the continent, Van der Meer was bound to continue their unprecedented journey together, no matter how tired one or both of them became. Besides, had he ever been required to give Clara away, the Protestant Dutchman would surely have preferred to ingratiate himself nearer to home in the Dutch Republic than to bestow Clara upon the Catholic French king. But had Louis XV been willing to buy Clara, Van der Meer was ready to conclude a transaction that made sense for both the seller and the sold. After all, had Louis bought Clara, she would have been installed in a permanent home and her prodigious consumption underwritten by one of Europe's wealthiest monarchs. To become the star attraction of the Versailles menagerie was not, after all, the worst fate that could befall an exotic animal in northern Europe.

The opening of the annual St Germain Fair in Paris on 3 February 1749 provided Van der Meer with the best of reasons for making a retreat from the court whilst preserving the dignity of all who had been party to the recent bargaining. Originally a trading benefit granted to a religious order, the fair had evolved throughout the eighteenth century into a dense grid of stalls interspersed with the sort of product demonstrations that will be familiar to anyone who has been to a large agricultural show or county fair. (Those who arrived in private carriages even received direction as to where to leave them in allotted parking areas.) Entertainment and refreshments to suit every taste and pocket completed a most popular way of spending a rare day's leisure in this temporary city within a city. The fair appealed to visitors of all classes, and in fact the experience of seeing Clara there is recorded in the diary of Casanova. From his first mention of Clara, it is apparent that all of the aristocrats with whom he was dining understood the reference to 'the rhinoceros' and that Van der Meer's scale of charges was very much public knowledge: 'Towards the end of the dinner, someone spoke of the rhinoceros, which was then shewn for twenty-four sous at the St Germain Fair. "Let us go and see it!" was the cry.'

Piling into their carriage, Casanova and his party reach the fair. Escorting two of his female companions through the thick of the crowd, Casanova has the opportunity to observe his current mistress walking in front of them:

At the end of the alley where we had been told that we would find the animal, there was a man placed to receive the money of the visitors. It is true that the man, dressed in the African fashion, was very dark and enormously stout, yet he had a human and very masculine form, and the beautiful marquise had no business to make a mistake. Nevertheless, the thoughtless young creature went up straight to him and said,

'Are you the rhinoceros, sir?'

'Go in, madam, go in.'

We were dying with laughing; and the marquise, when she had seen the animal, thought herself bound to apologize to the master; assuring him that she had never seen a rhinoceros in her life, and therefore he could not feel offended if she had made a mistake.

As the marquise displays what she takes to be her own great wit, the incidental detail offered by Casanova is telling. As he was a relentless traveller and socialite, it is unlikely that his reference to a dress 'in the African fashion' arises from his own ignorance of the differences between stereotypical Indian and African costumes. Van der Meer is not known to have darkened his skin artificially for the purpose of reinforcing Clara's exotic origins, neither is he ever described as 'enormously stout'. Casanova's diary therefore provides strong evidence that, at the St Germain Fair at least, Van der Meer hired a doorman who either may have been a genuine African or was simply made up to appear as one.

Clara was the first of her kind to be present in Paris within living memory, and she was the sensation of the St Germain Fair of 1749: just like those of any modern celebrity, the details of her appearance and preferences were impossible to escape. But how could Parisian society adapt its newfound knowledge of the species to the worlds of fashion and design? Which elegant aristocratic lady would wish to imitate a three-ton Indian rhinoceros?

Any director contemplating the staging of Eugene Ionesco's *Rhinocéros* (in which the inhabitants of a provincial French town experience a terrifying metamorphosis) must choose whether to encase the actors in realistic rhinoceros heads or to find a symbol immediately understood as visual shorthand for the presence of the animal. The most distinctive feature of any species of rhinoceros is, of course, its horn and it was a stylized representation of the horn that became the latest fashion accessory of the spring of 1749.

The Vicomtesse de Poillöue de Saint'Mars refers in her memoirs to ribbons '*à la rhinocéros*', suggesting perhaps the elaborate braiding of an upwardly coiffured woman's hairstyle. In a satirical poem of 1750 entitled 'Le Rhinocéros', J.-B. Guiard de Sevigné implies that as elaborate feathers signified the animal's horn, so a strategically placed cascade of silk ribbons would be read as symbolizing the animal's tail. Neither was fashion '*à la rhinocéros*' displayed only by humans: according to the poem, a gentleman fancying himself at the centre of the *beau monde* caused his carriage horses to be attired with both head feathers and tail ribbons, thereby transforming them into symbolic rhinoceroses.

Given that Sevigné's poem is a satire, it is easy to dismiss this last description as the poet's own comic invention, yet as late as 1787 the *Journal de Paris* can be found printing a letter on behalf of outraged pedestrians everywhere, claiming that one of their number had been run over by a carriage driven by two modish young men dressed as a macaw and a zebra respectively. To accessorize oneself or one's carriage horses as wild animals may indeed have been an eighteenth-century Parisian fashion, seen by its followers as allowing a degree of licence in their behaviour. If so, the long-established phallic connotations of animal horns would make the horn of the rhinoceros a particularly charged symbol in pleasure-seeking aristocratic circles. This would certainly explain Sevigné's reference to an unfaithful wife who smuggles her lover into the family home hidden in a cardboard rhinoceros.

The art historian T. H. Clarke has suggested that Sevigné's description of a life-sized model rhinoceros is an allusion to the Trojan Horse, but a more risqué possibility exists in another Greek myth, that of the Cretan queen Pasiphae, whose insatiable longing for a bull caused the inventor Daedalus to fashion a model cow in which she might be concealed and have her passion satisfied. As well as providing a genealogy for the mythical Minotaur, the story of Pasiphae and the bull confronts powerful taboos about social and moral codes. The rhinoceros lover described by Sevingé's poem may point us to one of a range of allusive meanings signalled by feathers and ribbons in Parisian society in 1749, for whilst these could simply have been innocent fashion accessories, they might also

have carried connotations of promiscuity, even sexual
insatiability.

Just as Clara inspired the production of a range of promotional goods, available to all income brackets and tastes,
so objects inspired by her – for example, fashion accessories – were capable of being variously interpreted,
according to the viewer's own knowledge and interests.
One thing was certain: Clara was a media phenomenon. As
the German writer Grimm neatly expressed it to Diderot:
'All Paris, so easily inebriated by small objects, is now busy
with a kind of animal called rhinoceros.' Clara was hardly a
'small' object, but her popularity nevertheless seems to
have confirmed Grimm in his view of the Parisians as
superficial, ceaselessly moving from one season's fashion to
the next. He would doubtless have found it ironic, then,
that out of Clara's residence in Paris would come two
enduring sets of monuments to her, representative of the
seemingly antithetical worlds of *objets d'art* and scientific
publishing.

Clara's residence in Paris was to inspire a set of exquisite
clocks which were produced in the 1750s and distinguished
by their use of specially commissioned models of her as a
base. The German Frankenthal clocks had used just a single model of Clara, but the French timepieces used one of
four representations of the rhinoceros. Throughout her
five-month stay in Paris in the spring of 1749, Clara must
therefore have been made available for a number of private

viewing and drawing sessions with some of the most skilled modellers working in the production of luxury goods. Van der Meer may have failed to extract 100,000 écus from Louis XV, but he would profit handsomely from each representation made of Clara.

It has been suggested that the images of Clara produced by Ridinger in Augsburg might have been of use to the Paris guildsmen involved in the production of such fashionable *objets d'art*. But the fact the modern eye might note similarities between Ridinger's work and that of mid-eighteenth-century Parisian model-makers does not mean that the latter worked with a copy of one or more of Ridinger's illustrations in front of them. It is more likely that the Parisian modellers, like Ridinger, availed themselves of the opportunity to sketch Clara for themselves. After all, who in Paris in 1749 would not have wished to go and see the famous rhinoceros?

The popularity of the Versailles menagerie and the regular display of exotic animals at Parisian fairs may perhaps explain the buoyant market for animal clocks in the reign of Louis XV. Whatever the species represented, the basic design invariably places the animal on an elaborate ormolu base, bearing the support of the clock upon its back. Providing a pyramidal structure to the whole, a gilt figure typically surmounts the clock, its nature often determined by that of the supporting animal. That such clocks were luxury artefacts, produced with high-status buyers in mind, is neatly illustrated in an oil painting of 1765 by Laurent Pécheux (now hanging in the Palazzo Pitti in Florence).

Pécheux's *Portrait of Maria Luisa of Bourbon-Parma* shows the granddaughter of Louis XV full length and in formal dress. Her head is turned to us but perhaps only momentarily, and the closed fan in her outstretched left hand invites us to examine the object that her body is angled towards and which she has plainly been studying. There on the console table, a model of Clara stands on an ormolu support, taking the weight of a clock that is almost the same height again. That Clara is the animal pictured cannot be in doubt: she was the only rhinoceros model available in Europe in the mid-eighteenth century and Parisian modellers, like their counterparts at Meissen, had quickly abandoned the Dürer archetype once knowledge of Clara became available.

A Louis XV bronze and ormolu rhinoceros clock based on Dürer's 1515 woodcut does exist (its lineage proclaimed by the presence of the entirely fictitious dorsal horn and elaborate concentric circles of drapery around the neck), but the specialist literature describing it for the antiques market is careful to specify '*c.*1749' as opposed to '1750s'. Like Johann Kaendler at the Meissen factory, the model-makers of Paris must have been taken aback when they first saw a rhinoceros with their own eyes. None the less, Clara duly became the model for all of the *pendules au rhinocéros* produced in Louis XV's reign.

Amongst this group of clocks, one signed on the white enamel dial by Noel Baltazar of Paris is of exceptionally fine quality. Clara stands as we have never seen her before: legs apart and head raised, she looks as though she is bellowing at some unseen aggressor and even about to charge. As many animal clocks were often accompanied by a *boîte à musique* and this clock has a musical movement by the master craftsman Viger, Clara's pose may be intended to generate a moment of comic incongruity as the only sound that escapes the whole mechanism is not the angry bellow of rhinoceros but the melodic chime of the movement. Clara's colouring, though rather too dark to be naturalistic, nevertheless provides a striking contrast with the gilt on which she stands and which flows over her back, anchoring the weight of the clock securely to its rhinoceros support. And the weight is not inconsiderable: the precision movement of Baltazar's clock is housed in a bronze case made by one of the leading bronze-founders in Paris at the time, Jean-Joseph de Saint-Germain. (The world of the craft guilds or *corporations* of Paris was strictly demarcated, but as a *maître-fondeur*, Saint-Germain enjoyed a special privilege: he was permitted to carry out work himself that would ordinarily have been undertaken by a member of an allied guild.)

The model of Clara that supports the clock appears to have been cast by Saint-Germain from a terracotta original produced in his own factory. Every craftsman involved in realizing some aspect of this work was an acknowledged master in his field, leading to the creation of a *pendule au rhinocéros* that was fit to grace a royal palace, even if it clearly differed from the clock pictured with Maria-Luisa of Bourbon-Parma. Surmounting the whole is a gilded figure whose rounded features and forearms recall the excess flesh typically found on cherubic infants in Western art. But this is no ordinary cherub, a range of whom are to be found up to mischief at the top of various animal clocks. This child carries a bow in his right hand and a quiver of arrows is visible above his left shoulder. His feathered headdress cements his identity as a native American Indian, yet this is puzzling. Figures symbolizing non-European cultures were often featured alongside Clara, but Baltazar's *pendule au rhinocéros* is the first time we see a representation of an American Indian with her. Was there any reason for Clara's identification with North or South America during her stay in Paris?

In 1757, when Giuseppe Zocchi painted his canvas *Allegory of America* (Il Museo dell'Opificio delle Pietre Dure, Florence), he pictured a female personification of North America, resplendent in feathered headdress, being drawn in a wagon pulled by a pair of rhinoceroses. (As Clara had by that time been seen in Italy, Zocchi's representation of the species is indebted to her and bears no hint of the Dürer dorsal horn.) Many explanations have been offered for the presence of rhinoceroses in European depictions of the Americas dating back to their earliest exploration. Most frequently, art historians suggest there was some confusion between the armour-plated armadillo of South America and the equally well-protected rhinoceros of Dürer's imagining.

Sir Walter Raleigh's *Discovery of the large, rich and bewtiful Empyre of Guiana* (1596) is often cited as aiding and abetting this confusion, Raleigh writing of his expedition to Central America that his party was in receipt of gifts including 'a beast called by the Spaniards Armadilla . . . which seemeth to be all barred over with small plates somewhat like to a Renocero'. But the operative words here are 'somewhat like'. Raleigh plainly does not confuse the two animals. Rather, the earliest depictions of Dürer-derived rhinoceroses in the North and South American landscapes seem to take their cue from descriptions likening the lands to a new Garden of Eden in which all species are presumably at the colonizers' disposal. But in the mid-eighteenth century, the association of the rhinoceros with North America can be traced to a specific group of texts introducing their readers to the latest thinking about what would today be termed 'evolution'.

In works by the Abbé Raynal and the Comte de Buffon, readers learned of great fossil bones found in America. Raynal refers to the fossilized evidence suggesting that elephants, rhinoceroses and other enormous quadrupeds once lived in America but now appeared to have vanished. Buffon tells of archaeological finds including the bones of elephants (presumably mammoths), the skeletons of rhinoceroses, the teeth of hippopotami and 'monstrous heads of cattle' (by which he may mean bison skulls). To both Raynal and Buffon, the fossil record seemed to offer evidence of unknown phases in Earth's history. It suggested not only that Earth was older than eighteenth-century church teaching allowed, following as it did biblical chronology, but also that species might inexplicably die out.

Raynal and Buffon had no concept of dinosaurs and so sought to understand reports of fossilized creatures in terms of existing animals, even if they did recognize that certain differences between modern and extinct specimens (often of size) were apparent. As the fossil evidence appeared to indicate that species of rhinoceros had once inhabited the North American continent, it was not incredible for artists to imagine that they might have been harnessed to chariots and put to work for the ancient inhabitants of the Americas.

The native American cherub brandishing his bow on top of the Baltazar *pendule au rhinoceros* of 1750 is therefore representative of the latest French understanding of North American natural history. Flawed though this interpretation of the evidence might be, it is nevertheless an imaginative translation of contemporary scientific knowledge into exquisite art. In 1749, as Clara did nothing other than to follow her ordinary routine, she was the unsuspecting focus of an extraordinary range of interest groups. The fashionable world accessorized hair, clothes and carriages in public confirmation of its fascination with her; the greatest craftsmen in Paris made drawings and models of her in order that she might be translated at a later date into a range of ostentatious *objets d'art*; and France's most famous thinkers argued about what Clara's presence taught them.

For Raynal and Buffon, creatures such as the elephant and the rhinoceros seemed to be living relatives of the massive fossilized remains discovered in the Americas. This invested the animals with a special status as ancient, primitive species. The opportunity to study a specimen of either at close quarters was therefore irresistible. It seems no accident, then, that Clara's visit to Paris in 1749 is immortalized in the two greatest publishing projects undertaken in eighteenth-century Europe: Diderot and d'Alembert's *Encyclopédie* (1751-72) and Buffon's *Histoire Naturelle* (1749-1804).

The contours of eighteenth-century French intellectual life were determined by the work of a diverse group of writers who lacked any common aesthetic, literary or political agenda. They were united only in their willingness to define themselves as *philosophes* and their belief in both the pursuit of truth and in the ability of scientific investigation to make the truth apparent. The hope of every contributor to the *Encyclopédie*'s twenty-eight volumes was that any reader should be able to reconstruct the whole of contemporary society and understand the latest state of knowledge on the basis of what was contained within its pages. Wherever possible, contributors were to report what they had themselves seen and could confirm to be true.

It is not surprising that the writer charged with producing the entry on 'Rhinocéros' eschews the many myths about the animal's behaviour that Van der Meer had incorporated so entertainingly into the text of various publicity posters. No assumptions are made about the longevity of the species and, for perhaps the first time, Pliny's doggedly persistent myth about enmity between the rhinoceros and the elephant is refined to suggest only that an enraged rhinoceros appears to have the strength to fight an elephant. Rather, the *Encyclopédiste* reports of the rhinoceros that it is a quadruped standing six feet high from the ground to the middle of its back, it is twelve feet long from nose to tail, and twelve feet in circumference, measured at the widest point of its girth. Since these are precisely the measurements given for Clara at reported public weigh-ins, the writer of this entry had either asked Van der Meer for Clara's vital statistics, or had enterprisingly approached her, tape measure in hand, in the true spirit of the *Encyclopédie*.

Clara had always acted as a corrective to Dürer's representation of the rhinoceros, and now she became the *Encyclopédie*'s archetype for her kind. Her dimensions established, the article proceeds to elaborate on her grey skin: the colour of an elephant, it is seen to be remarkable for the presence everywhere of tuberous swellings, except on the head and the neck, where great pleats of flesh are noted. The writer is careful to explain that the upper lip comes almost to a point and can therefore be used, like a finger, to grasp and pull at the grass that is a staple of the animal's diet. The novelty of this last observation cannot be over-emphasized: Indian rhino, like African black rhino, possess a remarkable prehensile upper lip that can snare leaves on overhanging branches. (In contrast, the African white rhino has a square mouth perfectly adapted for grazing the sub-Saharan plains. Indeed, the soubriquet 'white' is a corruption of the Afrikaans 'weit' meaning 'wide' – referring to the upper lip – and not 'white' as English settlers assumed.) Entirely in keeping with the spirit of the *Encyclopédie*, Clara's observer understands that her appearance may strike readers as fantastic, but this is no reason not to tell the truth.

Characterized as having tiny eyes and ears like those of a pig, Clara is anatomized from head to three-toed foot. In describing the most distinctive feature of the rhinoceros, the writer is clearly aware that the animal in front of him may not offer the most ostentatious example of a nasal horn. Some authors may have reported animals with two horns and readers may be expecting these to be of considerable length, but the writer insists he has evidence of only a single-horned rhinoceros, displaying a horn that is not even two feet in length. In every factual detail, the entry in the *Encyclopédie* describes Clara as she can be reconstructed from other contemporary descriptions. Since the multi-volume work did not begin publication until 1751, when Clara was already in Venice, and the *Encyclopédie* was not completed until twenty-one years later, the entry is a powerful reminder that anyone with a professional or personal interest in seeing a rhinoceros for themselves must have crowded to see Clara in the spring of 1749.

No one who saw Clara at the St Germain Fair had any expectation that they would ever see a live rhinoceros again. The *philosophes* were as aware of this as the working people who also queued to view her, but since it had been determined at an early stage in the production of the *Encyclopédie* that illustrations would be employed wherever they might prove useful, Diderot and d'Alembert were confident that they could provide a lasting reference point for what was otherwise mysterious and ephemeral. Their ambition was creditable: there was to be no recycling of old and inaccurate images. The *Encylopédie* would include an illustration of the rhinoceros that its text so accurately described. The result is an engraving of Clara, close up, in the spring of 1749: an image that one of the *Encyclopédistes* coveted for his own publishing purposes.

Georges-Louis Leclerc de Buffon was a wealthy aristocrat and Intendant of the Jardin du Roi or Royal Botanic Gardens in Paris. In 1749 he began to publish his monumental *Histoire Naturelle*, which eventually ran to some forty-four volumes. In seeking to classify the known animal kingdom, Buffon rejected the system established by the Swedish naturalist Linnaeus, one he believed to be too inflexible to take account of an infinitely surprising natural world. The illustrative plates so integral to the *Histoire Naturelle* allowed the viewer to envisage a range of exotic species and they imprinted on the mind more forcefully than description alone the new species being encountered by traders and explorers in Asia and the Americas. As the plates of the *Histoire Naturelle* circulated across Europe, being seen by a wider audience than those who could afford to buy even part of the whole work, their desirability was no doubt enhanced by murmurs of disapproval originating with the Catholic Church and given voice by the doctors of the Sorbonne. As represented in Buffon's volumes, the natural world raised more questions than the creation myth of Genesis seemed to answer. Yet beyond the ambition of its conception, the great goal of the *Histoire Naturelle* is one it shares with the *Encyclopédie*: its pursuit of truth. The natural world is drawn and described with as much fidelity as possible so that reflections upon it may be made on the basis of scrupulously accurate observation.

Like the *Encyclopédie*, the *Histoire Naturelle* uses a version of an engraving based upon an original painting of Clara by the celebrated artist Jean-Baptiste Oudry. Oudry held a special place in Louis XV's affections as the painter of the King's beloved hunting dogs, though his wider commissions included a full range of domestic and exotic animals as well as the obligatory still lives and aristocratic portraits. But Oudry's picture of Clara (now in Schwerin, Germany) is unique within the artist's canon, for it is a life-sized oil. The catalogue of the Parisian Salon of 1750 confirms the dimensions of the overall canvas (and therefore, indirectly, the dimensions of Clara in 1749): 'The Rhinoceros, life size, on a canvas fifteen feet long and ten feet high. This animal was painted in its pen at the St Germain Fair'.

Amusing though it is to imagine Oudry setting up a massive canvas at the fair, painting Clara *in situ* would have given him little opportunity to stand back and contemplate his work, and he would have been constantly interrupted by comments from the throng. Rather, Oudry must have negotiated with Van der Meer to be allowed to sketch Clara at certain pre-arranged times across several days. Some have insisted that Buffon commissioned Oudry, whilst Buffon himself maintained that Louis XV requested the painting be undertaken. It has even been suggested that Oudry painted the gigantic oil for his own pleasure. But as a favoured painter at court, Oudry had a strong sense of his own commercial worth, and he is unlikely to have devoted time to a work of such uncompromising scale that had not been contracted. Buffon's claim that Oudry worked to a royal mandate seems the most credible.

The series of paintings, *Chasses exotiques*, which Louis commissioned between 1735 and 1739 to adorn the Petite Galerie of the upper apartments at Versailles are all at least six feet by four feet in size, allowing the hunting of an elephant, leopard and tiger, among other species, to be represented to startling effect. Examples of all the animals in the series were kept in the royal menageries, and it therefore seems likely that, in expectation of arriving at some sort of agreement with Van der Meer, Louis might have commissioned Oudry early in January 1749 to make a life-sized painting of Clara, intending that it should adorn the galleried entrance to the Versailles menagerie. When relations soured between Van der Meer and the King, Oudry doubtless believed that the rift would prove temporary and Louis would still take possession of Clara. It is even possible that he thought his king might be happier with a life-sized representation of Clara rather than having to haggle over the flesh-and-blood original. But Louis appears to have been angered that Clara had slipped through his fingers and so, at the time of the Salon in 1750, Oudry still found himself in the inconvenient position of possessing a huge unwanted canvas that he had painted to a very particular specification.

In addition to the finished work, Oudry also had all of his preliminary sketches in chalk: a red chalk and a black-and-white chalk on blue paper (the latter now in the British Museum) are known, and it is likely that more exist. What was initially troublesome for Oudry proved, however, to be invaluable for a number of other artists who had been unable to capture Clara's likeness. The German painter Dietrich Findorff painted a *Rhinoceros after Oudry* at some time between 1750 and 1760 (now in the Staatliches Museum, Schwerin) whilst the English engraver Thomas Bewick relied on copies of Oudry's original to produce his own rhinoceros for *A General History of Quadrupeds* (1790). For his part, Buffon engaged the illustrator Jacques de Sève to copy and reduce Oudry's canvas, de Sève's handiwork then being engraved by Jean-Charles Baquoy for the *Histoire Naturelle*.

A single image of Clara, by Oudry, thus proliferated across Europe from the mid- to the late eighteenth century. Even though the *Histoire Naturelle* would only be completed in 1804 after Buffon's death, its plates circulated across the continent. Like the *Encyclopédie*, the *Histoire* is careful to stress that other sorts of rhinoceros have been reported – specifically, a two-horned variety and even creatures in possession of horns four feet long – but the text is supremely confident that these features are simply chance variants on the basic model described, or even embellishments of the truth. Through the *Encyclopédie* and the *Histoire Naturelle*, both of which utilized copies of Oudry's canvas of 1750, Clara had become the model not only for European conceptions of the Indian rhinoceros, but for rhinoceroses everywhere.

CHAPTER 7

Lying down with the Lion –
Carnival in Venice

'The animal swells like a bladder puffed with boozy
breath and collapses like a lung. Printers around the city
sell out their editions of Pliny's Natural History and print
more which sell out too.'
Lawrence Norfolk, *The Pope's Rhinoceros*

Though Clara's tour of France had begun badly, with
Louis XV taking affront at Van der Meer's unwilling-
ness to donate the only rhinoceros in Europe to the royal
menagerie, it had ended in triumph, with Clara's likeness
influencing the worlds of fashion and science. Van der
Meer now had two choices: to enjoy a period of rest or to
capitalize further on Clara's extraordinary success. As she
continued to appear to be in good health, he chose to
keep her firmly in the public eye, heading for Naples and

Rome before entering Venice at the height of Carnival.

Any tour of Italy that concluded in Venice necessarily involved the repeated transfer of Clara between ship and shore. But what if there were to be reports that Clara had met with some misfortune at sea? Might not public concern about her fate result in a huge demand to see her alive and well? After all, the citizens of Rome would be especially vulnerable to the suggestion that the ship carrying Clara had sunk, for was not this the same misfortune that had befallen the animal immortalized by Dürer as it sailed from Lisbon to a new home in the Papal Gardens? Yet it was Venice that attracted Van der Meer even more than Rome. The city was a magnet for European travellers at any time, and its population swelled during Carnival as visitors indulged themselves in an extended masquerade of fancy dress and libidinous behaviour, encouraged by a local population who understood that tourism was already a significant part of the city's economy. There could surely be no more appropriate venue in which to disseminate a quite unsubstantiated rumour about Clara.

Whilst a stay in Venice during Carnival seemed a natural culmination of Clara's Italian tour, the decision to tour Italy was a politically complex one. In 1749, two significant mainland European markets remained untested for rhino-mania: the Iberian and the Italian peninsulas. An Indian rhinoceros had already been brought to Europe in 1515 and again in 1579 by the Portuguese monarchy, which might therefore have been interested to receive a visit from Clara. But reaching Portugal by sea from the Netherlands involved navigating the stomach-churning currents of the Bay of Biscay, and Van der Meer had no intention of risking Clara in such notoriously treacherous waters. Had Clara undertaken a Spanish tour, Portugal could easily have been fitted into her itinerary, but Van der Meer's was never going to take Clara to Spain, however profitable the visit might have been.

Like any other Dutch citizen, Van der Meer would have loathed Spain and her imperial ambitions. In 1482, the Spanish Crown had claimed the Low Countries, establishing a strategic presence for its empire in northern Europe. Since the Spanish Crown was one of the many titles claimed by the powerful Habsburg family, by far the greatest number of wars fought on European soil from the fifteenth to the eighteenth centuries were intended to keep Habsburg power in check. In 1585, Elizabeth I of England sent forces to assist Dutch Protestants in liberating themselves from the occupying Spanish army, leading to the creation of the United Provinces: a Dutch republic that maintained its fiercely independent Protestant identity with the wealth generated by its far-flung trading empire.

From spice islands in the Far East to the swampy and unprepossessing island of Manhattan, Dutch traders came to control some of the most lucrative and strategically significant outposts of European empire. Dutch economic success in the eighteenth century had not, however, obliterated memories handed down through families of the atrocities and hardships suffered by the Dutch under Spanish occupation. Van der Meer may have been content to pay his respects to the Austrian branch of the Habsburg dynasty in the person of the Empress Maria Theresa, but the thought of requesting the favour of the Spanish monarchy was repellent to any self-respecting Dutchman. Furthermore, following the withdrawal of Louis XV's interest from Clara's tour of France, Van der Meer almost certainly had no wish to risk repeating the experience of a royal misunderstanding with the mercurial Ferdinand VI of Spain.

In contrast to the long-established nation states of Portugal and Spain, eighteenth-century Italy was, as the Austrian statesman Metternich would remark in 1849, 'a geographical expression': a collection of principalities where, should Van der Meer lose the favour of one prince, a neighbouring ruler would be sure to display a different temperament. Italy was not simply the better option; it was the only one Van der Meer could countenance.

In November 1749, Clara sailed from the port of Marseilles for Naples: an unremarkable event in itself, but a miraculous occurrence given a contemporary report that she had killed 'five or six persons' in Lyons, before dying from a rage which had been caused by sexual frustration.

(Thanks to the preservation of the rumour in the memoirs of the Marquis d'Argenson, the impact of the news is possible to gauge – the Marquis thinking it worthwhile to include details about '*le rhinocéros*' in his journal.)

The premature announcement of Clara's death – and its supposed cause – can be explained in a number of ways. The simplest interpretation is that her predictable hormonal mood swings were much in evidence when Clara was displayed in Lyons. Perhaps she was not her usual placid self, and as many of the crowd judged it wise to leave, rumours spread that something terrible had happened. To link Clara's subsequent death with sexual frustration certainly seems bizarre, although two factors may have determined that this became Clara's rumoured fate.

Many of the exotic animals displayed across Europe at the time were single specimens, causing naturalists to speculate at length about their breeding habits. For artists and writers, a lack of scientific facts was no barrier to suggesting a range of improbable, not to mention physically unfeasible, behaviour. The prolific eighteenth-century French writer Restif de la Bretonne offers one of the more perverse accounts of reproduction techniques in his novel *La Découverte australe* (1781), where the vast southern continent is supposed to be populated by a collection of animal–human hybrids. Aware of contemporary (but erroneous) reports that elephants bred with the male on top of the female, face to face, Restif illustrated his elephant–human hybrids in all their full-fronted nakedness, water gushing from both the male's and female's upright trunks. Speculation about the rhinoceros's reproductive urges was just as rife. Furthermore, the rhinoceros had long been linked with ideas of sexual potency, mainly through the aphrodisiac and phallic associations of its horn. Rumours that Clara had died from sexual frustration were not surprising, then: as she very obviously lacked a mate, Clara was assumed to be suffering.

Two more rumours were to surface of Clara's premature demise. In November 1749, the German paper *Auszug der neuesten Weltgeschicte* reported the overturning of the small vessel transporting Clara from the quayside of Marseilles out to a waiting sailing ship. Since ship design at the time did not allow for any loading ramp that might compromise the structural integrity of the hull, men had to get aboard ship via ladders or narrow gangways. All cargo, including animals, had to be hoisted on board, and this was usually done close to shore or dockside, where winches were available. Men could have been taken out to their ship in a smaller boat, and often were, but never a rhinoceros.

The German story was neither probable nor possible. It was, however, considerably less dramatic than the other rumour concerning Clara's fate (again preserved by the Marquis d'Argenson). As the ship taking her down the western Italian seaboard passed Rome on its way to

Naples, stories began circulating that the vessel had been lost in spectacular fashion. Clara was reported drowned, and Van der Meer had supposedly sunk beneath the waves as he struggled to recover, or was weighed down by, the bags of money that had fallen overboard.

One false report of Clara's death is perhaps unfortunate, yet three in succession start to take on the appearance of a deliberate policy. At every stage of Clara's tour, Van der Meer tried to introduce some variation into the experience of viewing Clara and the expectations it encouraged. Once her wagon had rolled through the Holy Roman Empire, a pattern of a sort had been established, but it risked inducing public apathy if repeated too often. So the visit to the Swiss cantons and lower Rhine had incorporated the great river itself into her travels and display. In Paris, Clara had unwittingly managed to be all things to all viewers so the tour could make a virtue of its own temporary stasis, giving both the fashionable and the philosophical worlds time to observe her at close quarters. And now that Clara was expected in Italy, where fashionable society could not bear to be thought lagging behind Paris, what could be more crushing to public expectation than one report after another of her recent death? The only way to distinguish truth from falsehood, rumour from counter-rumour, was to see Clara in the flesh.

If Van der Meer was responsible for all of these premature obituaries – and it seems far from implausible, given his track record – then it was a stroke of genius on his part: media manipulation of the most brilliant kind. The ruse worked because it recalled the drowning of the Lisbon rhinoceros and therefore tapped into an unarticulated but probably widespread belief that, if the king of Portugal could not deliver a rhinoceros to the Pope, fate did not intend such an animal to land on Italian shores. As news spread from Naples that Clara had in fact been brought safely to land, the aristocratic appetite to see her grew insatiable. If she had survived a near-drowning (or three), the deliverance was nothing short of miraculous. Clara had never been so popular.

In late November 1749, Clara was the subject of an oil painting by an unknown artist entitled *The Rhinoceros in its Booth near the Castelnuovo, Naples* (now in the collection of the Duke of Wellington). The 'booth' is represented as a large loose box in which a small crowd of spectators stands within a few feet of Clara, separated from her only by an improvised wooden rail that looks as though it would yield to even the slightest pressure. An expensively dressed gentleman in a suit of red stands in the foreground, trying to get as close to Clara as possible: of the many reactions she inspired in the viewing public, fear was not one. That art historians should have identified the man in red as an aristocrat or adviser to the court only emphasizes the readiness of Italian society figures to be seen with Clara, who now enjoyed the status of an international celebrity.

Clara appears to have stayed in Naples for three months, since the next reported sighting (in the Roman journal, the *Diario ordinario*) places her in the Holy City in the first week of March 1750. Then, as now, Rome drew pilgrims from all over the world, spawning a host of ancillary services to cater to both their spiritual and physical needs. Some of Van der Meer's earliest broadsheet publications advertising Clara's display had been careful to emphasize that buying a ticket to see her was not merely a frivolous indulgence but an opportunity to reflect on the mysterious ways of the Creator as evinced in the strangeness of the created world. This publicity angle could now be reworked for the Roman market and the idea of viewing Clara sold to the pilgrims not as simple entertainment but as an aid to spiritual reflection in the Holy City itself. Similarly, the popularity of her tour was undoubtedly helped by the public knowledge that a former Pope had wanted a rhinoceros for the Papal Gardens. If a pontiff had actively sought to acquire such an animal, there could be nothing wrong in paying for the privilege of seeing one. From March to June, Clara drew significant crowds and traded the jolting of her wagon for a roomy display pen with abundant quantities of water, bread and hay to hand. Then, in June, something wholly unexpected happened. Clara shed her horn.

The phenomenon has been observed since rhinoceroses were first held in captivity, and continues to frustrate modern zoo keepers. In the wild, rhinoceroses are not observed to shed their horns, leading to fierce argument about the conditions of their captivity. So do captive animals rub off their horns as part of the repetitive behaviour patterns noted in many captive species, just as we might bite our finger-nails in similar circumstances? Are such behaviour patterns expressive of boredom or stress? Does captivity make the rhinoceros more prone to fungal and other infections that result in the loss of the horn? We simply do not know.

Once the horn is shed, it will grow again from the base. But for Van der Meer, Clara's loss of her horn, no doubt through her repeatedly rubbing it against wooden surfaces, presented a marketing problem. The public paid him in the expectation that they would see an exotic horned ani-mal, and their only guarantee that Clara grew a horn was its daily presence on the end of her nose. For perhaps the first time in his life with Clara, Van der Meer was at a loss to know what to do.

The rarity of the rhinoceros in Europe at the time had helped to make Clara famous and sought after, but those charged with the care of exotic animals brought to Europe – giraffes, for example, tigers and sea lions – had little or no information about what was normal for a particular species. An obvious physical change might be significant, or it might mean nothing at all. In June 1750, Van der Meer had no body of literature to advise him: Clara appeared to be her usual self, but the loss of her horn simply could not be ignored.

If the possibility that something was seriously wrong with Clara occurred to Van der Meer, it also occurred to Clara's legion of Roman fans. Perhaps the rhinoceros was dying. Perhaps the Roman crowds would be the last to see her. In Florence, Clara was expected daily, but as if in imitation of an aristrocratic lady, she showed apparent disregard for arrangements and bookings already made. Correspondence from English residents in Florence at the time indicates the high levels of anticipation in the city that Clara would soon arrive – and the collective sense of frustration that she did not.

As early as May 1750, Sir Horace Mann confided to his good friend, Sir Horace Walpole, that Florentine women were obsessed with the fashion for dressing hair '*à la rhinocéros*, which all our ladies here follow, so that the preceding *mode à la comète* is only for . . . antiquated beauties'. Through May and June, society women exhorted their hairdressers to pay stylistic homage to the eagerly expected visitor, unaware that Clara had lost the very attribute their fashions were intended to recall. As June shaded into July, and July sweltered into August, disappointment gave way to despair among Florentine fashion setters: the rhinoceros did not come. Perhaps it was dead. Perhaps it had never existed. Perhaps hair *à la rhinocéros* was really not so elegant. And yet it was rumoured that the extraordinary creature had entered Bologna in a carriage drawn by twelve oxen. If Clara continued to head north, this could mean only one thing: she was sure to end up in Venice during Carnival. If Clara could not go to Florence, perhaps Florentine society could go to Clara. Perhaps hair *à la rhinocéros* was still the height of fashion after all.

The rumours circulating in Florence about Clara's appearance in Bologna from mid-August to early September were true, and since there are no known sightings of her in between Rome and Bologna, it is likely that Van der Meer took passage for them on a ship sailing north. Paradoxically, the confines of a ship would have both given the Dutchman space and time in which to think and temporarily remove Clara from the public gaze. By the time they had reached Bologna, Van der Meer had obviously decided to come out fighting.

The Italian theatre historian Corrado Ricci records that Clara entered the city in a large wagon, drawn not by the usual complement of eight horses but by six pairs of oxen. As we know that Clara's wagon was covered and did not allow expectant crowds to see her, Van der Meer's decision to swap the horse team for twelve oxen worked to his advantage in two distinct but related ways. Firstly, as the oxen pulled in tandem, the wagon likely travelled much more slowly than when harnessed to a horse team: the wagon's slow but stately progress therefore gave ample proof of the extraordinary weight of what it contained. Those watching her entrance into the city immediately endowed Clara with the attributes of size and weight before thinking about the details of her appearance (and size and weight were something that a viewing of her would still deliver, despite the loss of her horn). Secondly, the team of oxen displayed twelve fine pairs of horns between them. If the image of these horns registered in the mind of anyone watching Clara's wagon enter the city, it would no doubt reassert itself at some subliminal level when they saw Clara herself: horns, real or imagined, would remain very much a part of the whole experience.

Van der Meer could not have achieved the same affect with a horse team and, to his immense satisfaction and relief, the ploy generated huge public interest. So great was the demand for viewings of Clara and souvenirs that a consignment of medals with an Italian inscription sold out and Ricci tells us that the only medals that could finally be had were tin and inscribed in French. At some point on the French tour, Van der Meer must have taken delivery of a batch of relatively cheap tin commemorative items, a small quantity of which remained unsold as the French public tended to prefer wares of better quality. The citizens of Bologna must clearly have thought the tin French medals to be better than none at all, and Van der Meer enjoyed a rapid turnover of stock.

Clara was so different to anything the inhabitants of Bologna had seen that her lack of a horn did not deter viewers: if anything, the possibility that Clara was ailing, the loss of her horn the most visible symptom of this, seemed to generate a great amount of sympathy. If Van der Meer did not concern himself with the abstract debates of anatomists, naturalists and theologians concerning Clara, he always took the keenest interest in the general public's response to events on the Tour. The behaviour of the Italian public must have now reinforced his previous observations that people were grateful to find Clara alive when they had believed her to be dead or ailing. Three times in the last year, Clara and Van der Meer had been reported drowned; each time they had surfaced to give the lie to the rumour, and each time the crowds had been bigger than ever. The loss of the horn, which had initially seemed to herald the end of the Tour, had instead provoked a huge amount of interest and speculation.

If Van der Meer had orchestrated some or all of these rumours, he now had the chance to direct events on the largest stage-set in eighteenth-century Europe: Venice during Carnival. It is a commonplace of histories of Venice and its most famous residents to note that the eighteenth-century city was already a shadow of its former self. The tourists who flocked there to gaze on its gorgeous Renaissance façades were generally unaware of the decay and squalor into which many residents perceived the city to be sinking. For Venice's long-established aristocratic families, the decline was exemplified by the ennoblement of the wealthiest merchants and traders simply in order to maintain numbers among the enfranchised patrician class.

For her citizens, the decline was evident in the unwilling-
ness of the surviving noble families to patronize artists and
craftsmen as their ancestors had once done. Already in the
eighteenth century, Venetians of all classes shared a per-
ception that the erstwhile Queen of the Adriatic now
depended upon foreign wealth and benevolence to sustain
her ageing frame.

Indeed, only the need to generate huge amounts of
income could explain how the Venetian Carnival had
grown into the biggest annual party in Europe and one that
regularly lasted half the year. From the first Sunday in
October until the Christian remembrance of Lent, Venice
seemed to play host to a city-wide masquerade. For the
tourists who disguised themselves in fancy dress and the
itinerant performers who tried to separate them from their
money, there was an unreal quality to the whole: for ordinary Venetians, it was vital that this insubstantial play was
sustained, for it generated very real wealth. For anyone
who could engage and manipulate the interest of Carnival-
goers, the rewards were potentially enormous.

It was widely rumoured that Van der Meer and his wonderful creature would arrive in Venice in early January
1751. Clara had never displayed any anxiety about travelling by water and the prospect of taking her into the city by
barge did not give Van der Meer any undue concern. Clara
could simply be winched onto one of the quaysides where
men and machinery daily handled imports by the ton. But

in a city swarming with tourists from other parts of Italy and from further afield, it was somehow inevitable that rumours of Clara's drowning would now resurface.

Venetian gossip was all too ready to believe that a dreadful accident had happened as Clara was being transferred from barge to quay and that she had fallen into the waters of the lagoon. Beside himself, Van der Meer had offered any amount of money to anyone who could secure a hoist about Clara and thus keep her afloat. So men, even as they feared the bulk of the distressed animal, had jumped into the canal, tempted by Van der Meer's reward. But had they survived? And, anyway, was it possible to save a rhinoceros under such circumstances? The 'five or six persons' whom Clara had supposedly killed in Lyons were now an integral part of the lore surrounding the tour and these wholly fictitious deaths were readily appropriated by those describing Clara's drowning in Venice. Unsurprisingly, when she was discovered to be alive and well, Venetians and visitors alike queued to see the creature that had so recently cheated death. Here was an advertising campaign that relied not on engravings or medals but on people's readiness to repeat and confuse existing stories, adding elaborations to them all the while.

The crowds that queued to see Clara in Venice in January and February 1751 are recorded in greater detail than those at any other point of the Tour, chiefly in the oil paintings and etchings of the father and son, Pietro and

Alessandro Longhi. Out of at least eight known illustrations of Clara's time in Venice, the most intriguing are undoubtedly two closely related canvases by Pietro Longhi. *The Rhinoceros in Venice* (1751), in the possession of the Ca'Rezzonico, Venice, and the *Exhibition of a Rhinoceros at Venice* (1751), on display at the National Gallery, London, both show essentially the same scene. Clara stands in the centre of a wooden enclosure, eating hay. She is conspicuously lacking her horn, which is held up for display by a young man in a tricorn hat at the left of the canvas. Though often identified as Van der Meer himself, the man's angular face bears little relation to the rounded features of the sea captain to be found on a selection of the publicity broadsheets. It therefore seems more likely that the horn-holder pictured by Longhi is the young man employed as Van der Meer's assistant. To the right of the assistant and on graduated benches behind him, there are seven figures, while at the far right of the Venetian version of the canvas, a notice is shown on the wall, stating the painting to be 'a true portrait of the rhinoceros brought to Venice in 1751 and painted by Pietro Longhi as a commission from the nobleman Giovanni Grimani dei Servi: Venetian Patrician'.

There are other, more striking differences between the two paintings. On the canvas that can be seen in Venice, the only mask-wearers are the man seen to the immediate right of the young woman in the front row, and the woman who stands at the apex of the picture. On the canvas at the National Gallery, masks have been added to all of the men in the front row, with the exception of Van der Meer's assistant. Comparing the two canvases and the identical stances of all the figures involved, a viewer will rapidly arrive at the conclusion that the picture in the National Gallery is perhaps the marginally later of the two, representing a reworking or over-painting of a sketch that is the original of both Pietro Longhi canvases.

In masking three additional figures in the second canvas, and removing the explanatory notice on the wall to the viewer's right, Longhi is conventionally held to be illustrating the intrigues of Carnival and the festival's showcasing of exotica, in both animal and human form. On closer inspection of the London canvas, however, it is apparent that Longhi has done more than capture a typical day in Clara's display. In the *Exhibition of a Rhinoceros at Venice*, Longhi uses the conditions of Clara's captivity to comment on the lives of aristocratic Venetians around him.

The London canvas was also commissioned by a nobleman, Girolamo Mocenigo, but he clearly had no wish to proclaim his patronage within the frame of the painting itself. Mocenigo therefore becomes one of the many identities withheld from the viewer of the painting. Indeed, the only individual who conceals nothing from us in the canvas is Clara herself: turning away from the painter, she continues eating and producing the piles of dung that are so evident in the foreground. In the front row behind her, three of the spectators wear the *bauta*, a white mask that could be worn by either men or women. Close up, it is a shock to realize that the *bauta* wearers on either side of the richly dressed young woman have been painted to show their eyes riveted on her rather than on Clara. As they hem her in, she stares out at the viewer, make-up rendering her face every bit as white as the *bauta* itself. In the front row, only Van der Meer's assistant is open-mouthed, but he too seems to be more interested in doing rather than saying, for his left index finger points at Clara.

In the second row, another young woman stands between two other viewers. She wears the *domino*, an oval black mask kept in place by a button held between the teeth, an arrangement which rendered its wearer temporarily speechless. At her side, an older woman has briefly removed her own *domino*. In these figures, we perhaps see what the tightly corseted little girl who stands with them will herself become: a woman who cannot speak for herself and who is judged initially by her appearance alone, like the gorgeously dressed young woman who stands mute in the front row, boxed in by her male admirers. In wearing the fashionable *domino*, the women of Venice render themselves as dumb as Clara and, like Clara, are judged solely by their appearance, their true natures hidden beneath the accoutrements of a city-wide masquerade.

Since the nobleman Girolamo Mocenigo who commissioned Longhi must have agreed to the details to be included in the picture, one can use the evidence provided by all these figures to guess at the patron's motivation. As the young woman in the front row confidently returns the painter's gaze – she is the only figure on the canvas to stare straight out of it – it is impossible to escape a sense that she shares an affinity with Clara, for both are creatures on display. Was the woman the object of Mocenigo's affections or obsession? Given that the first version of the picture, now in Venice, was commissioned by another nobleman, Giovanni Grimani dei Servi, did both men have a shared interest in the human enigma at the centre of their canvases? When Mocenigo placed Longhi's canvas on his wall, did he see Clara as its exotic subject, or did he see himself as regulating access to the young woman, just as Van der Meer controlled the display of Clara?

Whatever the answers to these questions, Longhi's paintings of Clara executed in 1751 are much more than faithful records of the Venetian crowds who came to marvel at the rhinoceros. Rather, they pose complex questions about the relationship between appearance and reality, men and women, ownership and freedom. That these questions were asked in a city where disguise was *de rigueur* and nothing was as it seemed only serves to entangle Clara still further in a complex web of private allusions on what is now a very public canvas.

One thing is certain, however: for sophisticated Venetian Carnival-goers, the experience of seeing Clara, and seeing pictures of themselves viewing Clara, was full of meaning. Following the contemporary success of *Exhibition of a Rhinoceros at Venice*, Pietro Longhi would execute commissions for pictures including elephants and lions also displayed in Venice. Always these exotic animals are surrounded by *bauta*-wearers and the odd individual who dares to show his or her face, posing uncomfortable questions about who, or what, was really on display in a city whose life blood was the masquerade.

Where Pietro Longhi seems to have worked to a very specific brief for his patrons, including details in his canvases to meet their exacting demands, his son Alessandro preferred to situate Clara among the performers and freaks of Carnival. Six etchings of Alessandro's from 1751 show actors dressed in costumes that were instantly recognizable to Italians as representing figures of the *commedia dell'arte*. The street theatre with which these figures were associated embraced the familiar characters of Harlequin and Punchinello, whose English incarnation, 'Mr Punch', continues to display the bewildering mixture of comedy and cruelty that characterized *commedia dell'arte* performances. In the etching *Il gran Rinoceronte* (1751), Alessandro Longhi borrows the scene already established by his father in the two commissions for Venetian noblemen: Clara stands in her wooden booth, only now she faces to the left, rather than to the right. In the front row of spectators, immediately above her, Van der Meer's assistant displays her shed horn in his outstretched left hand. A young woman immediately behind him has just removed her *domino*.

There the similarity between the pictures of father and son ends. To the right of Alessandro's etching, a clown from the *commedia dell'arte* stands staring at Clara. His true expression is impossible to read, for he wears the mask of Punchinello, a favourite with the Venetian gentry and one whose grotesque nose was conventionally understood as a phallic symbol. From Punchinello's head, a conical hat of between two and three feet tall rises above the heads of the crowd and towers over Clara's horn, which Van der Meer's assistant is waving in the air. It is as if Punchinello has been inviting Carnival-goers to compare his mock horns (both nose and hat) with Clara's real one, and to find Clara wanting. But now that he stands staring at her, he is disquieted. Clara has her massive back turned towards him, and as she eats her way through a pile of hay, so she drops her dung only inches from his feet.

In this game of one-upmanship, Alessandro Longhi shows us that Clara will always be the victor: the longer we stare at the clown, the more ridiculous and pathetic he appears. Like Clara, he is used to being stared at, but unlike Clara, he is not indifferent to the responses of the crowd around him and they have come to see '*il gran rinoceronte*', as great a draw as ever even despite the loss of her horn. Without his stage props, Punchinello is nothing: despite Van der Meer's initial fears, Clara could lose the defining attribute of a rhinoceros and still be a crowd-pleaser.

The text beneath Alessandro Longhi's etching proclaims Clara to be '*il gran Rinoceronte . . . Dall' Africa*'. As no Italian state of the time pursued an imperial agenda in Asia, and Italian rulers were accustomed to obtaining their exotica from North Africa, Longhi's confusion regarding Clara's origins is perhaps understandable. It could, however, confirm an earlier suggestion regarding the make-up of Van der Meer's entourage at this stage in the tour. Amongst the most popular costumes of Carnival were stereotypical Western interpretations of African, Chinese and Turkish dress, and we know that, when Clara was displayed in Paris, Casanova's mistress thought the doorman to whom she spoke was African. Perhaps Longhi imagined Clara's origins to be African because Van der Meer had retained the services of his African doorman from the St Germain Fair. In the atmosphere of Carnival, with the European aristocracy wild for all manner of African and oriental costumes, Van der Meer might have thought it a shrewd marketing ploy to station an African doorman in authentic dress at the entrance to Clara's enclosure.

The use of Clara in paintings and etchings examining Venetian society was not simply confined to the Longhis' studio, however. In imitation of Alessandro Longhi's etchings, an anonymous Venetian painting from the same decade shows Clara with the so-called 'Irish giant', Magrath, one of scores of men and women who travelled Europe eking out a living from making a spectacle of their own bodies. Where Petrus Camper had drawn and modelled Clara as part of a scientific investigation into comparative anatomy, the anonymous artist constructs a cruder visual comparison of his own between Clara's three-ton bulk and Magrath's grossly distended body. (Now in the possession of Trinity College, Dublin, Magrath's skeleton shows his height to have been seven feet ten.) Like Pietro and Alessandro Longhi before him, this painter uses the conditions of Clara's display to comment upon the way in which men and women display themselves and allow themselves to be looked at on a daily basis. Sometimes, the canvases seem to imply, their human subjects have little more freedom than Clara herself.

If Venetians of all classes caught glimpses of themselves in pictures illustrating this leg of Clara's Italian tour, and if Clara's popularity generated a clamour for the display of more exotic imports in the city, the fashion for matching human and animal subjects in complex allusive canvases was to backfire in a poignant way in 1762. The symbol of Venice is the Lion of St Mark. (The Evangelist is traditionally symbolized by a lion as he opens his Gospel with an account of Christ and St John the Baptist in the wilderness, inviting his readers to recall lines from Genesis in which Christ is called 'the Lion of the tribe of Judah'.) In countless artistic and literary representations, the Lion of St Mark is terrifying in its power and majesty. Conscious of the huge success of Clara's visit to the city, and the revenue generated by her display, the ruling council thought it appropriate to license the display of a lion in St Mark's Square in 1762. But the animal was so tame that it seemed to mock its namesake, and for many contemporary commentators and subsequent historians of Venice, the poor beast only seemed to emphasize the fact that this was a once mighty power in real decline.

After Clara's visit of 1751, no other exotic imported animal could quite live up to Venetian expectations, but then no other import was promoted as Van der Meer had promoted Clara. She had been the talking point of Carnival and the only exhibit that it was absolutely necessary for any man or woman of fashion to see. Van der Meer did not need to outstay the duration of the festivities. He had exhausted supplies of even the tin medals inscribed in French and of all his posters. It was time for another period of rest and recuperation in Leiden, and the decision to return home was to prove momentous in Van der Meer's private life. He would marry and his wife would bear him a child. It would, of course, be a girl.

CHAPTER 8

Ready Rhino – A Last Bow in London

'Johnson's laugh was as remarkable as any circumstance in
his manner. It was a kind of good-humoured growl. Tom Davies
described it drolly enough: "He laughs like a rhinoceros."'

James Boswell, *Life of Johnson* (1791)

When Clara and Van der Meer left Venice at the close
of Carnival in 1751, they had already spent ten years
together. Van der Meer's experience was unprecedented,
and it remains unrepeated. It therefore seems entirely
appropriate that questions about the effect of Clara's Tour
on its participants had been anticipated and partially
answered by one of the eighteenth century's great fictional
travelogues.

In Jonathan Swift's *Gulliver's Travels* (1726), Gulliver's
wife and growing family are mentioned only in passing, as
Gulliver temporarily returns home from his travels. At the

conclusion of the book, Gulliver's greatest wish is to please his Houyhnhnm (or horse) master. Exiled from Houyhnhnm land, he feels he has more in common with the residents of his stable than the wife and children who are unfamiliar to him – and his preference for animal over human company leads his neighbours to conclude that he is mad.

By 1751, Van der Meer was altogether better placed than the unknown Dutch East India Company employee who had returned home to Leiden at the age of thirty-six with a tame rhinoceros. He was now wealthy and famous. But where other men kept horses in their stables, Van der Meer kept Clara, and like the fictional Gulliver, he had spent longer on his improbable travels than he had spent in any one place. As a calf, Clara had imprinted on the people around her, and had learned to see Van der Meer in particular as her source of daily sustenance and affection. Uncomfortable though it might have been for Van der Meer to acknowledge, Clara was *his* chief companion, and her success the source of his wealth and esteem. What place was there in this relationship for anyone else?

The known facts of Van der Meer's private life are sparse. Between his birth on 12 April 1705 and his decision to leave the employ of the Dutch East Indian Company in 1741 (when he returned from India with Clara), he appears to merit no mention in official records. The date of his marriage to Elisabeth Snel is not recorded, but on 5 December

1751 their daughter, Elisabeth, was baptised in the Pieterskerk in Leiden. (A modern chronicler of European rhinomania, L. C. Rookmaaker, observes, apparently without irony, that Clara's whereabouts are not known at the time of the baptism.) As there is no record of any child of Van der Meer's being baptized earlier than Elisabeth, she appears to have been the couple's firstborn, and it is therefore probable that Van der Meer married Elisabeth Snel very shortly after his return from Venice.

If this was the case, Elisabeth must have known all about Van der Meer's somewhat unusual lifestyle when she married him after only the briefest of courtships. Her family were, however, unlikely to have demanded any details of the occupation of their daughter's suitor, for Van der Meer and his sizeable fortune were by now famous throughout Europe. In making Van der Meer wealthy, Clara had also made him highly sought after in the marriage market and, whilst he had no need to seek a woman who brought with her a substantial dowry, it is extremely unlikely he would have chosen a pauper with equally needy relatives eager to profit from Clara's fame.

Nothing is known about Elisabeth Snel beyond the simple facts recorded in the Leiden archives, but it is possible to gauge a great deal about her character from the trajectory of Clara's tour in 1751 and immediately afterwards. Whereas Lemuel Gulliver's fictional wife had little influence over her husband's repeated decisions to embark upon another journey, Elisabeth appears to have resisted being left at home in Leiden during her pregnancy and as a new mother. From 1752 to 1754, there are no documents or artefacts to indicate that Van der Meer took Clara anywhere. The triumph of Venice was not capitalized upon in the way that previous successes had been, providing momentum for the next stage of the Tour.

Regardless of what his wife asked of him, the decision to remain in Leiden must have made economic sense to Van der Meer. If Clara were kept comfortably stabled in Leiden for one or two years, she could re-grow her horn, while it was as good as guaranteed that her absence from the public arena would only heighten interest in her when she returned to it. Once again, Van der Meer's decision proved an excellent media strategy, and it is a measure of his wealth that he could afford to feed Clara's gargantuan appetite for two years without feeling the need to display her once during this time.

After 1754, the details of Clara's whereabouts become erratic, although, to a greater or lesser extent, this is true of many of her travels. Confusion often abounds in the written record. For example, a poster referring to Clara's visit to Leipzig in 1747 makes Clara male. While in Paris in 1749, Clara was described for the scientific community in Ladvocat's *Lettre sur le rhinocéros*, but as Ladvocat is massively indebted to an item by James Parsons in the *Philosophical Transactions* of the Royal Society of London –

a letter of 9 June 1743 discussing a male rhinoceros present in London from 1739 to 1741 – what is ostensibly a report about Clara is not necessarily an accurate reflection of her behaviour or appearance at the time.

From the sixteenth to the eighteenth centuries, a similar pattern emerges in texts discussing all of Europe's imported Indian rhinoceroses. Writers and artists who were unable to see a specimen for themselves appropriated the reports of others and relied on hearsay to produce 'true' accounts of incidents that never happened, while typographical errors, all too easily made, sometimes resulted in erroneous dates being given for Clara's presence in various places.

Clara may none the less have toured Poland in 1754 and Denmark in 1755. Isolated pieces of evidence suggest that she visited Warsaw and Cracow in 1754, and the Danish king, Frederik, certainly gave permission to Van der Meer to exhibit Clara in Copenhagen in June 1755. Beyond this, however, little is known. No documentary trail has been established indicating where Clara might have stopped *en route*, though tours of both Poland and Denmark would have necessitated a journey through the northern German states. But what is not open to question is that, later in the decade, Van der Meer decided to introduce Clara to the most important market that remained to him: England.

At each stage of her Tour, public and professional interest in Clara had generated a range of products –

broadsheets, clocks, encyclopaedia entries, engravings, fashion accessories, medals, *objets d'art*, paintings, poems, statues and theological tracts. What distinguishes the English stage of the tour is the preponderance of literary references to Clara, indicating not only that she had been seen by some of the most influential writers of the age, but also that they could assume their audiences would understand allusions to her.

The impact of Clara upon the English viewing public can be gauged by James Boswell's recollection of a conversation he had with a London bookseller about the mannerisms of their mutual friend, Samuel Johnson. In his entry for 17 May 1775, Boswell notes: 'Johnson's laugh was as remarkable as any circumstance in his manner. It was a kind of good-humoured growl. Tom Davies described it drolly enough: "He laughs like a rhinoceros."' This is not a standard simile of the English language. Indeed, it does not bear any sort of close scrutiny: what, after all, might a laughing rhinoceros look or sound like? Yet as there was no rhinoceros to be seen on English soil from Clara's visit, which concluded in 1758, until a male animal was displayed in 1790, Davies's only exposure to the species must have been when he viewed Clara at some point in the late 1750s. And since Davies thought his comment intelligible in 1775, a full seventeen years after Clara was last displayed in London, she had clearly had a profound impact upon those who queued to see her. Davies was not, however, the only one among Johnson's circle of friends who was so affected.

Oliver Goldsmith is perhaps best known today for his sentimental novel, *The Vicar of Wakefield* (1766), but in his lifetime the struggling author turned his hand to every kind of text in an attempt to keep creditors from the door. In 1752, the twenty-four-year-old Goldsmith had surprised those closest to him by his decision to spend some time in Leiden, only returning to England in 1756. The professors at the University of Leiden enjoyed an international reputation at the time, and Goldsmith was undoubtedly attracted by the prospect of becoming a student once more. And that he availed himself of the opportunity to see Clara in either Leiden or London – or perhaps in both places – is evident from one of his least-known but most influential works: *An History of the Earth and Animated Nature* (1774).

Goldsmith's eight-volume work of natural history was a long time in the planning. By his own account, he had initially intended a straightforward translation of Pliny's *Natural History*, the classical study that originated the widespread belief that the elephant and rhinoceros were mortal enemies. But after he had reread Pliny, Goldsmith eagerly began to consume Buffon's *Histoire Naturelle* as its first three volumes rolled off the presses from 1749 onwards. The *Histoire* changed for ever Goldsmith's conception of good natural history: where Pliny had collected together the beliefs of others, Buffon reported what he and his team of collaborators had seen.

Determined that the English-speaking world should have its own comprehensive reference work of natural history, Goldsmith began what was to be a decades-long process of collecting data for his *History of the Earth and Animated Nature.* The original eight-volume work was to be reprinted, abridged, updated and shamelessly plundered throughout the nineteenth century as over twenty editions were put into circulation. For many Victorian families across the British Empire, Goldsmith's *History* became the authoritative reference work, and as Clara was the only specimen described in the entry for the rhinoceros, her inclusion in the text ensured she also set the pattern for nineteenth-century conceptions of her species.

Goldsmith places his discussion of the rhinoceros immediately after an account of the elephant, thus recalling Pliny even as he corrects the Roman writer's misconceptions. After only a few lines of Goldsmith's description, the influence of Buffon and the *Encyclopédistes* is apparent: 'Next to the elephant, the rhinoceros is the most powerful of animals. It is usually found twelve feet long from the tip of the nose to the insertion of the tail; from six to seven feet high; and the circumference of its body is nearly equal to its length.' It is not that Goldsmith plagiarizes texts by his French counterparts. Both the *Histoire Naturelle* and the *Encyclopédie* give these dimensions for the rhinoceros because those responsible for the relevant entries have observed and measured Clara: twelve feet long, six feet high, and almost twelve feet round, these are her vital statistics in the 1750s, as confirmed from broadsheets and medals reporting the results of her public weigh-ins. But Goldsmith had both seen Clara himself and researched what had already been written about her. This much is clear from the following passage:

But though the rhinoceros is thus formidable by nature, yet imagination has not failed to exert itself, in adding to its terrors. The scent is said to be most exquisite; and it is affirmed that it consorts with the tiger. It is reported also, that when it has overturned a man, or any other animal, it continues to lick the flesh quite from the bone with its tongue, which is said to be extremely rough. All this, however, is fabulous: the scent, if we may judge from the expansion of the olfactory nerves, is not greater than that of a hog, which we know to be indifferent; it keeps company with the tiger, only because they both frequent watery places in the burning climates where they are bred; and as to its rough tongue, that is so far from the truth, that no animal of near its size has so soft a one. I have often felt it myself, says Ladvocat, in his description of the animal; it is smooth, soft, and small, like that of a dog; and to the feel it appears as if one passed the hand over velvet; I have often seen it lick a young man's face who kept it, and both seemed pleased with the action.

*

Here Goldsmith rehearses beliefs about the rhinoceros only to show them to be false. Reports about the animal's smell are belied by the experience of his own nose, while myths about relations between the rhinoceros and tiger are explained in terms of behavioural necessity in climates where fresh water is in short supply. Quoting Ladvocat's *Lettre sur le rhinocéros*, written after the Frenchman had seen Clara displayed in Paris in 1749, Goldsmith uses Ladvocat's memorable description of Clara's velvety tongue to introduce a remarkable image, that of Clara licking Van der Meer's face in front of at least one astonished witness. Even if Clara was simply responding to the smell of tobacco permeating Van der Meer's clothes and hair, or to the scent of an orange he may have been holding, the Dutchman was clearly confident that he was not in any danger from her massive canine teeth.

Although the boundaries between Ladvocat's observations and Goldsmith's own are blurred towards the end of this passage (in contrast to Goldsmith's earlier refutation of beliefs about the animal's smell, judged from his own experience), as the entry progresses, it becomes apparent that Goldsmith has talked to Van der Meer in detail about Clara's habits. Confirming that Van der Meer really believed Clara might live for one hundred years, Goldsmith tells us that Van der Meer gave out she was 'eighteen years old, and even at that age he pretended to consider it as a young one'. Adamant that the rhinoceros is a herbivore, Goldsmith tells his readers, 'It is particularly fond of the prickly branches of trees, and is seen to feed upon such thorny shrubs as would be dangerous to other animals, either to gather or to swallow.' There is no precedent for this description of the wide range of vegetation preferred by all species of rhinoceros: certainly there is nothing similar in Pliny's *Natural History*, Buffon's *Histoire Naturelle* or Diderot and D'Alembert's *Encyclopédie*. Goldsmith had researched his subject thoroughly and was determined to describe what he had learned, even if it contradicted all that his readers already believed to be true.

For at least one of Goldsmith's Victorian editors, however, the most important observations that had been made of Clara were those of Petrus Camper, who had used his first-hand experience of examining Clara's horn to argue that the unicorn was an anatomical impossibility. An edition of Goldsmith's *History* published in 1840 by Blackie and Sons of Glasgow 'with numerous notes, from the works of the most distinguished British and foreign naturalists' takes issue with Camper's work. Referring to the six-year studies of a Mr Edward Ruppell in north-east Africa, the reader is told that Ruppell had seen bones of an antelope-like creature which seemed to display a single prominent cranial horn, and that 'the anomalous position of this appendage furnishes a complete refutation of the theory of Camper with regard to the unicorn, that such an occurrence was contrary to nature, and proves at least the possibility of the existence of such an animal'. The text also insists that another Victorian amateur naturalist, a Mr Hodgson, had found evidence of 'the chiru, or unicorn of the Himalayah Mountains'.

The modern reader may well wonder why a Victorian reprinting of Goldsmith's work was so determined to refute Camper's conclusions, yet in insisting upon the existence of unicorns, Ruppell, Hodgson and their editor are merely showing their true creationist colours. The King James Bible had long since replaced all reference to the unwieldy rhinoceros with the elegant yet elusive unicorn, and in so doing it had presented Victorians who insisted upon the literal truth of the Bible with something of a problem: where could they find evidence of the unicorn's existence? It was hardly surprising, then, that such umbrage was taken at an eighteenth-century anatomist whose argument was, in essence at any rate, proto-Darwinian. Camper had been right to suggest that the graceful unicorn of myth could not exist: not even Clara's massive bulk could sustain a weight of bone upon the head. But Victorian creationists did not wish to dismiss a menagerie of such mythical creatures – not least because the fabled appearance of these creatures provided a ready-made explanation for some of the more bizarre skeletal remains now being unearthed by fossil-hunters.

When Van der Meer had first displayed Clara, he teased the public that some believed her to be the Behemoth of the Book of Job. To a number of nineteenth-century thinkers, there was reassurance in this thought. Where Goldsmith had striven to understand the truth about the animals he saw, and had tried to see as much as he could of the natural world at first hand, some of his Victorian editors were distinctly more comfortable with Clara as a starting point for rehearsing myths about Behemoth or the unicorn.

Continually appropriated by scientists, theologians and artists for their own purposes, Clara's image, which had been effectively copyrighted by Van der Meer during her lifetime and his, was to be freely adapted and transmitted across the British empire thanks to Goldsmith's *History*. And whilst the particulars of the illustrations used would change across the work's various incarnations, the text would remain the same: wherever Goldsmith's *History* went, there was Clara, licking Van der Meer's face in a demonstration of the complete trust that had developed between man and rhinoceros.

Goldsmith would not live to see the success of his natural history. He died in the year of its first publication, 1774, one year before the bookseller Tom Davies would compare their mutual friend Samuel Johnson to a laughing rhinoceros, and seventeen years before Boswell would publish the observation in his *Life of Johnson* (1791). Any assertion about Clara's popularity in England and the fact that she had given the species a lasting recognition factor must therefore be weighed against the tightness of the

199

intellectual circles in which Goldsmith, Davies and Boswell moved. It is unsurprising to find men of letters demonstrating the currency of their knowledge of the natural world. It is extraordinary, though, to find a middle-class writer revising his greatest fictional work to take account of Clara's immense contemporary popularity.

Samuel Richardson was a successful London printer and temperamentally averse to what he regarded as immoral novels aimed primarily at an innocent and impressionable female readership. In response to the request of a group of fellow printers, he wrote what he thought was a morally instructive tale about a virtuous servant girl who resists her wealthy master's attempts to seduce her, finally gaining a proposal of marriage from him. *Pamela, or Virtue Rewarded* (1740–41) was a multi-volume sensation that propelled Richardson to literary fame across Europe. Members of the clergy encouraged their congregations to buy the text, though aspirant female readers likely bought it for reasons other than moral instruction.

Concerned that some of his readers aspired only to earthly gratification, Richardson followed *Pamela* with a 1,500-page tragedy in *Clarissa* (1747–8). His theme is once again the attempted seduction of a virtuous young woman, but here the plot leads not to understanding between the protagonists and marriage, but to imprisonment, rape and death. The architect of Clarissa's downfall is the libertine, Lovelace. Even as the first instalments of *Clarissa* rolled off the presses in 1747, some readers warned Richardson that Lovelace was dangerously attractive. He was horrified and immediately embarked upon revisions to his text, the instant success of which had already necessitated additional printings. By 1759, ten years after its first complete issue, *Clarissa* was circulating in four different editions that had each been updated in the course of their printing.

For the bibliographer, the task of establishing the precise date at which Richardson made revisions to the work is daunting, since various editions of the multi-volume work were all in circulation during his lifetime, some substantially revised. The longest novel in the English language is also one of its most protean, but what is certain is that the first edition does not include a reference to Clara that was present in the fourth edition of 1759. In this, the last edition to be published during Richardson's lifetime, Lovelace expresses his frustration with what he regards as his sister Charlotte's primness and writes to his friend, Belford: 'She really is a dainty girl. And thou art such a clumsy fellow in thy person, that I should as soon have wished her a Rhinoceros for a husband, as thee. But, poor little dears! they must stay till their time's come! They won't have this man, and they won't have that man, from Seventeen to Twenty-five.'

Clearly, Richardson thought 'a Rhinoceros' to be a suitably witty comparison for a fashionable man like Lovelace to make, but he must also have thought the reference comprehensible to his adoring female readers. Richardson was not a writer given to excluding sections of his readership, even for a moment. In expecting that his readers, both male and female, would be able to envisage the bulk of a rhinoceros, he tells us a great deal about the popularity of Clara among her London audiences.

That Clara appeared on the London stage in 1758 is therefore established beyond doubt. There are also assertions that she was displayed in London in both 1751 and 1752. In support of an appearance in 1751, there is a report in the highly respected *Gentleman's Magazine* (for December 1751) claiming that a display of 'natural curiosities' in the capital included 'a female rhinoceros, or true unicorn'. A drawing by George Edwards, published in the *Gleanings of Natural History* (1758), claims to be representation of 'the female rhinoceros, drawn from the life in London, A.D. 1752'. The latter would be more credible had not previous commentators been embarrassed to point out that Edwards preserves a convention whereby early natural history illustrators showed details of an animal's anatomy separate from the main body of the creature. To the left of his 'female rhinoceros', Edwards has drawn the animal's penis, in order that his interested eighteenth-century gentlemen readers might not have to wonder what it was like. Since this is a feature of illustrations of the male rhinoceros exhibited in London from 1739-41, Edwards is clearly borrowing and synthesizing at will.

Van der Meer may well have intended to make a visit to
London in the early 1750s, but if all competing claims for
his activities are taken at face value, the years 1751 and
1752 would have been the most intensive stage of Clara's
Tour, with visits to Frankfurt, London, Prague and Vienna
– not to mention a stay in Verona after the Venetian
Carnival. An itinerary of sorts can be constructed that satis-
fies all those who claimed a visit from Clara in the early
1750s, but it is not a convincing one. Besides, it is very difficult to imagine that a measured progress through
Germany, Austria, Switzerland, France and Italy that took
five years to complete should suddenly have given way to
a frantic series of journeys as far apart as the Czech
Republic and England, all compressed into a two-year
space when Van der Meer also married and became a
father. What is much more likely is that Van der Meer
wrote ahead, obtaining permission to show Clara in various
towns, and then, as his private circumstances changed, he
decided that he could after all afford to stay a little longer
in his comfortable new home, with his equally new wife
and child. Despite all the false reports of Clara in the 1750s,
however, it is certain that, after a period of display within
Holland itself, Van der Meer brought Clara to London in
1758. This is unassailable, for it was there that she died.

Van der Meer seems to have had no inkling of Clara's
death. There is no reason to suppose that he did not
believe his own publicity that the rhinoceros lived for a

203

hundred years. A good life expectancy for a captive rhinoceros today would be forty years, but it is impossible to say whether Clara might have lived longer had she led a different life. The publicity printed for the 1758 visit to London does not refer to any apparent illness of Clara's that Van der Meer could have turned to a marketing advantage. On the contrary, Clara is represented in the best of conditions: 'to be seen, at The Horse and Groom in Lambeth-Market, the surprising, great and noble animal called Rinoceros alive'. The last qualifier, 'alive', does not indicate that Van der Meer had any special cause for concern. Rather, this substantiates suggestions that a model animal, or even a crudely stuffed version of the 1739-41 rhinoceros, was being displayed in the English provinces. (Taxidermy was in its infancy, however, and a preserved animal could not have lasted in good condition for any length of time.)

After reminding prospective viewers that 'a great many people' think the rhinoceros to be the Behemoth of the Book of Job, the broadsheet goes on to stress that Clara is 'the only one of that kind in all Europe, and of such a wonderful shape, that the wisdom and power of the Creator of these animals appears in it with all brightness and splendour'. After familiar claims about a natural enmity with the elephant, a propensity to dive like a duck, and a reference to the 'dominions of the great Mogul', we receive assurance that Clara's appetite was healthy:

The said animal consumes every day seventy pounds of hay, and twenty-five pounds of bread, and drinks fourteen pints of water: it is at present eighteen years of age, twelve feet thick, and six thousand pounds weight. The royal family and the nobility and gentry have seen this animal with great admiration and satisfaction. This creature may be seen from eight o'clock in the morning, till six in the evening, even if there is but one person at a time, so that nobody need to wait, at one shilling the first place, and sixpence the second. It is to be seen in a tent, where there is a way for coaches to come up.

References to 'the first place' would seem to indicate a ringside vantage point, in contrast to a second row of spectators who paid less for a less advantageous view. Despite the claim that Clara would remain on display for the advertised hours, even if viewers came singly (or not at all), the fact that the royal family and court had seen Clara would have been enough to guarantee high levels of ticket sales – and Van der Meer is unlikely to have made the claim of royal approval had it not been true.

Unsurprisingly, Clara became as a great a talking point in London as she had been in any other European capital. But then, inexplicably, we read in a German version of the broadsheets sold by Van der Meer that Clara died in London on 14 April 1758. For once, reports of her death were not exaggerated.

Assuming she was approximately two years old when purchased by Van der Meer in India and brought to Leiden in 1741, Clara would have been no more than twenty in 1758. Since there are no contemporary reports from visitors surprised by any visible signs of illness, whatever caused Clara's death was sudden and wholly unexpected. Yet to blame Van der Meer for it seems unreasonable. Clara may after all have succumbed to a disease that would have killed her in the wild in exactly the same silent way and at just this age. Alternatively, the vast quantities of bread she consumed whilst on display in London may provide a clue, since any fungal growth in the wheat could, if consumed in sufficiently large quantities, have had a severe effect on even Clara's robust digestive system. But we will never know. All that can be stated with any certainty is that, at the time of her death, Clara was the longest-lived rhinoceros in captivity in Europe and the most influential there has ever been in terms of fixing an accurate representation of the animal in the European mind.

For Van der Meer, Clara's death must have been deeply shocking, and he would have felt the loss all the more sharply since none could share his emotions. How could anyone else understand the extraordinary journey that had been Clara's Grand Tour? For seventeen years, Van der Meer had moved freely across social boundaries and state borders, courtesy of a travelling companion unique in history. Since 1741 his daily routine – and that of any assistants he had employed – had been determined by Clara and her needs alone. Now all this would change, the men would have to be paid off and any remaining memorabilia sold. There was also the pressing question of what to do with Clara's body. Death is inevitably followed by decay. When the showman P. T. Barnum lost his prize elephant, Jumbo, in 1885, he rapidly decided that death was no barrier to continued exhibition and had the stuffed skin mounted and displayed alongside the massive skeleton as a macabre sort of 'double Jumbo'. In 1758, though, there was no taxidermist who had the skill to preserve Clara's body, no repository where the body might be preserved on ice whilst Van der Meer considered what to do with it – and a fully grown Indian rhinoceros with rigor mortis cannot simply be buried in the countryside under cover of darkness.

In life, Clara had walked wherever and whenever she was required to. In death, she was a rigidly immovable three-ton weight. But just as her public display had begun with the sketches of an anatomist's engraver, so it is likely that an anatomy lesson served as a more private end to her long career. From rudimentary networks of medical practitioners to groups of amateur scientists, London was home to a good number of men who would have relished the chance to dissect a dead rhinoceros and learn all that could be established about the creature's anatomy before the body was too badly decayed. If this seems a cruel fate for Clara's corpse, it should perhaps be remembered that the ability of Europeans to keep future captive rhinoceroses alive and well depended upon an increased understanding of the animal's physiology.

Without either ceremony or publicity, Clara's body must have been given to some of those anxious to take any opportunity to learn more about the fundamental workings of the natural world. Regarded by many with abhorrence, anatomists were likely to keep details of their activities largely to themselves. When a tiger died at Pidcock's London menagerie in the 1780s, the great painter of equine anatomy, George Stubbs, went to Pidcock's under cover of darkness (at 10 p.m.) and found to his delight that the body was his for three guineas. Exotic animals were prized in their lifetimes but disposed of in desperation on their deaths.

Clara can lay claim to no autopsy or obituary. The report of her death and the lack of any subsequent display are the only evidence of what occurred – and if there was significantly less interest in Clara's death than in her life, this can perhaps be explained by the simple fact that she had never been expected to live even half as long as she had: her death at eighteen, possibly twenty, was not a source of disappointment but one of amazement.

Finally stripped of its flesh, Clara's skeleton would none the less have remained unusual enough in 1758 to merit safe-keeping. Were the records of the period more detailed, it might be possible to point to Clara's bones in one of the museums in the south of England that today hold early modern rhinoceros skeletons. But the most likely candidates for Clara's resting place are generally unable to confirm the precise date at which a particular skeleton came into their care. Given that two different Indian rhinoceroses would be displayed, briefly, in London from 1790 to 1793 and in 1799, attempts to identify a particular set of Indian rhinoceros remains as Clara's need more evidence than is currently available. As for Van der Meer, after leaving Clara's body in London, he returned home to Leiden and simply disappears from the written record. One can only presume that the Tour had left him rich enough to live on its profits for the rest of his life.

In colloquial English, 'rhino' is slang for money. The first examples in literature of the word being used in this way are to be found in the seventeenth century, with many further examples occurring in eighteenth-century English drama. Playwright Thomas Shadwell records five separate uses of the term in *The Squire of Alsatia* (1688), the most flamboyant outburst being the most explanatory: 'Money. The Ready, the Rhino; thou shalt be Rhinocerical.' Nearly a hundred years later, another playwright, Edward Thompson, has a character in *The Fair Quaker* (1775) lament, 'Where's the rhino to come from?' Dictionaries of popular phrases agree that 'rhino' as a colloquialism for money must refer to the high price commanded by rhino horn: European seamen quickly understood this was a prized trading commodity in the East, and it was through their accounts of overseas trade that the term entered the English language. But although this explanation may point to the term's possible origin, it need not represent the whole story. As Clara's history shows, a rhinoceros itself was a valuable commodity in early modern Europe, and it is events that took place after Clara's London visit in 1758 that may well account for the continued colloquial use of 'rhino'.

In 1787, the official coin of the realm in England was in desperately short supply: this was not a matter of inflationary economics but of the mint being unable to meet basic needs. A variety of token coins therefore appeared in circulation mocking the mint's inadequacy, imitating the tradition of commemorative medals and serving as an advertising tool for enterprising businessmen. Gilbert Pidcock, owner of the Exeter Change menagerie in The Strand (on a site now covered by Burleigh Street), issued at least two token halfpennies showing an Indian rhinoceros, whilst an enterprising apothecary brought out his own token coinage showing an Indian rhinoceros advertising the curative properties of 'Sir Samuel Hannay's original, genuine & only infallible' medicine. Just as Clara's image had once graced commemorative medals in the Rhineland, so she now circulated in place of coins of the realm: 'ready rhino' indeed.

Anxious to repeat Van der Meer's success, Pidcock

unsuccessfully imported two Indian rhinoceroses to London, but one survived only from 1790 to 1793 and the other for less than twelve months in 1799. Poignantly, the walls of Pidcock's Exeter Change menagerie were painted with the very exotica that he tried in vain to display, including the 'true unicorn' or rhinoceros. In the last decade of the eighteenth century, the rhinoceros was still considered a unique attraction, worth acquiring by anyone who aspired to make a significant income from showing wild animals. Such had been Clara's extraordinary impact.

Clara may long since have been reduced to a set of skeletal remains, currently gathering dust in some London museum, but in a very real sense she is still physically present in our culture. Before her, only a handful of early modern Europeans had seen an Indian rhinoceros. Many believed the animal to be a myth. Those who had seen – and faithfully reproduced – a copy of Dürer's 1515 engraving, *Rhinoceros*, were unaware that they saw a beast in armour rather than an armour-plated beast. But as Clara toured eighteenth-century Europe, and as images of her proliferated in a variety of media and permeated European culture, she became the archetypal rhinoceros. Few animals have ever had such an impact and changed for ever the way in which we see and understand their species. This, then, is Clara's achievement and, finally, her obituary.

Epilogue

Today there are five species of rhinoceros that survive: the Sumatran, the Javan, the Indian, the African white and African black rhino. Given that only 300 Sumatran rhino are currently known to exist, and a mere sixty Javan animals, it may not be long before these species are declared extinct. According to the International Rhino Federation, the Indian rhino would then be the most endangered, its present population being 2,400 animals. Africa's black rhino population remains prey to poachers who value the horn for its ornamental and supposed aphrodisiac properties and smuggle it to markets in the Middle and Far East, but Africa's black and white rhino populations have both attracted huge interest in comparison to the three species of Asian rhino, and with populations of 3,100 and 11,670 respectively, they may yet avoid extinction for many years.

Where early twentieth-century farmers in South Africa allowed big game hunters to slaughter up to five hundred rhino a day to clear the giant herbivores from grazing land, the farmers' descendants now pay as much as £50,000 per animal to re-stock their land with rhino, as the rhinoceros is one of the most treasured trophies to be shot at close quarters, but by the camera lens. In KwaZulu–Natal, the Hluhlowe–Umfolozi game reserve has been so successful at breeding African white rhino (with five thousand bred since the 1960s) that the park now holds regular wildlife auctions of surplus stock, attracting bids from those who wish to diversify from farming into eco-tourism.

Unlike the early white settlers who thought the rhinoceros a giant pest, today's African farmers recognize that rhino, unlike lions, can be grazed with cattle and are actually good for business. Yet as Umfolozoi becomes a conservation success story, it highlights how much needs to be done to bring other rhinoceros populations anywhere near this level. The game reserve reflects both our similarity to and difference from Clara's eighteenth-century audience. Like them, we are ready to stand in wonder at the difference of the natural world. Unlike them, we find it increasingly desirable to see wild animals *in situ* – a desire that seems to become more pronounced as the pressure on the world's wild places becomes ever greater. Where Clara's eighteenth-century audience paid a few shillings to see a live rhinoceros face to face, their descendants will pay thousands of pounds to repeat the experience in the animal's own environment.

It is estimated that, at the start of the twentieth century, the Indian rhinoceros population had been allowed to dwindle to under two hundred animals. That approximately twelve times that number survive today is clearly encouraging. Indeed, Indian states are becoming more alert to the potential for developing wildlife tourism, using tourist dollars to keep Indian rhino where some would say they belong, in the Assam sanctuaries of Kaziranga National Park, Manas, and Orang. Perhaps, then, the Indian rhinoceros will never again be as rare as it appeared to Europeans from the sixteenth to the eighteenth centuries, a period from which there are two great survivors: Clara herself, immortalized across the European arts, and one other.

Even among the many attractions of Paris, the Muséum National d'Histoire Naturelle in the Jardin des Plantes has much to recommend it. From the entrance level, the visitor walks up a storey, gradually emerging into the Grande Galerie de l'Evolution, where the animals of Africa are represented streaming through the heart of the building. From this interior savannah, complete with African rhino, the visitor can appreciate both the design of the building and the luxury of space in its hollow centre, with all the galleries above this floor level clinging to the walls of the building. From these second and third levels, the visitor gains new vantage points on the display below, as well as access to more dimly lit rooms: galleries filled with species long since extinct, and those that are more recent casualties of Earth's changing conditions.

The top floor of the museum includes some of its oldest specimens on display and here, in a corner dedicated to eighteenth-century French natural history, is a stuffed rhinoceros. Three-quarters of the body is afforded the protection of a clear display housing, in the corner of which a monitor constantly checks the surrounding atmosphere. Emerging from its oversize kennel, only the animal's head and shoulders are available to close scrutiny, even as a rail indicates that visitors should keep a suitable distance from the exhibit. Despite the fact that explanatory notices within the display case reproduce one of Van der Meer's broadside illustrations for Clara's Tour, this is not Clara. Instead, it is what she might have become had Louis XV been willing to buy her from Van der Meer for 100,000 écus. For this is the rhinoceros that was presented to the Versailles menagerie in 1770 and whose travel requirements ran up such a huge wheelwrights' bill.

Louis's rhinoceros appears to have been smaller than Clara. The skin looks unnaturally hard in places, even allowing for the thickness of the hide, and the visitor can be forgiven for harbouring a suspicion that the original animal is not entirely 'there'. Although the oldest example of ornithological taxidermy (the Duchess of Richmond's

African Grey Parrot in Westminster Abbey, London) dates from 1702, the discipline was then in its infancy and animals were not widely preserved. It was not until the 1770s that a French apothecary, Jean-Baptiste Becoeur, developed an arsenic-based paste that worked to preserve large animal skins. But Becoeur guarded his secret formula jealously and only in 1820 was it made commercially available by another French taxidermist, Louis Dufresnse.

In fact, the Paris rhinoceros is something of an enigma: the survival of any part of the original creature is astonishing, and yet however unnatural the animal appears, it gives us a real sense of what eighteenth-century spectators must have felt as they marvelled at a living rhinoceros. Here, after all, is the animal that was eventually housed in that part of the royal menagerie intended for Clara and that, after the Revolution, came to the bars of its cage to be scratched by Buffon as he strolled through the derelict royal gardens.

The continuing restoration and updating of the galleries in the Jardin des Plantes reminds us that each generation sees the past through a different lens. The taxonomic hierarchies of Victorian museum displays have been replaced with narratives about man's impact upon the world's ecosystems. Where nineteenth-century spectators gazed on isolated specimens of exotica, early twenty-first-century viewers are prompted to consider complex questions about man's relationship to the natural world, and even to ponder why man has historically taken pleasure in the display of other species.

Museums are not the only institutions to register changing attitudes. Zoos the world over wrestle with problems that would have been inconceivable to Clara's viewing public. When Van der Meer displayed her, she was typically shown in a wooden pen containing as much water and hay as she wished. With the notable exception of the time she spent in the Orangery at Kassel, no attempt was made to replicate the conditions of her native habitat. Indeed, for eighteen years, Van der Meer travelled with Clara across the primitive coaching roads of Europe, and her home was essentially a wooden crate on wheels. And in all the debate she inspired, no eighteenth-century commentator thought it appropriate to ask whether Clara *ought* to be displayed or treated in this manner.

It is important, though, to remember what brought people to see Clara. The modern visitor who fails to see a particular animal at the zoo has no sense that it will remain for ever a mystery: he or she can always come back and see it another time, or watch a programme about it on television. But when Clara stopped in a particular town, her display offered local people the only chance they thought they would ever have to see a rhinoceros. Which of us promised a single opportunity to see a recreated woolly mammoth or an extra-terrestrial life form would not join the queue? In her lifetime, Clara was as fantastical a subject of display as either a prehistoric animal or an alien being would be now.

In 1741, without any professional help or specialized guidance, an unknown Dutch sea captain decided that his future prospects might improve radically if he brought a young, female Indian rhinoceros back to Europe and displayed her. He was right: Clara's story captivated a eighteenth-century viewing public of all classes and nationalities and made her owner an extremely wealthy man. But over two and hundred and fifty years later, it is not Van der Meer's earnings that interest us: it is the potency of his original idea and the nature of his – and hence our – relationship with Clara.

Of all the images of Clara we have inherited, there is perhaps one that best reflects the great wonder she generated and fed – a wonder that is still very much part of us. It is that description in Goldsmith's *History of the Earth and Animated Nature*. Douwemout Van der Meer stands in front of Clara and, to the delight of all concerned, is licked by her velvety tongue in a display of complete trust – or, at the very least, a demonstration of her lifelong partiality to the smell of tobacco or the scent of oranges.

Further Reading

Some topics mentioned only in passing in this book have a sizeable literature of their own — for example, the myth of the unicorn and Dürer's conception of the rhinoceros. The list of sources is not intended as a guide to the best reference works on these distinct topics, but rather to books and articles that have direct bearing on *Clara's Grand Tour*. All of the rhinoceroses imported into Europe from the sixteenth to the eighteenth centuries have been discussed in the works of T. H. Clarke and L. C. Rookmaaker. Key works by these writers are listed below. The reader who consults works by Clarke and Rookmaaker will find itineraries for Clara's touring: the preceding text agrees with some of Clarke's and Rookmaaker's proposed itineraries (which do not always agree with each other) and disagrees — silently — with others. I have not drawn attention to areas of agreement or disagreement with either of these writers in the text, since they and I are ultimately reliant on the same source material (often conflicting), and are confronted by the existence of the same artefacts. No one has previously considered the totality of Clara's journey in any detail and attempted to account for the best substantiated facts about her tour. The conclusions of *Clara's Grand Tour* are my own. If this book leads anyone to search for further information about parts of the Tour, it is quite likely that additional information and previously unknown illustrations are waiting to be found, in local archives and museums across Europe. If and when such material is found, I shall be happy to acknowledge any preceding errors as my own also.

Altick, Richard D., *The Shows of London* (Cambridge, Mass. and London, 1978)

Bartrum, Giulia, *Albrecht Dürer and his Legacy* (London: The British Museum Press, 2002)

Beeson, David, *Maupertuis: an intellectual biography* (Oxford: Voltaire Foundation, 1992)

Clarke, T. H., *The Rhinoceros from Dürer to Stubbs: 1515–1799* (London: Sotheby's, 1986)

Emmerig, Hubert, 'Das Rhinozeros in Europa 1741–58 und seine Medaillen', *Money Trend*, vol. 10, no. 5, pp. 20–25, 50, 52

Gesner, Conradus, *The History of Four-Footed Beasts and Serpents . . . Collected out of the Writings of Conradus Gesner and other Authors* By Edward Topsel (London: E. Cotes for G. Sawbridge T. Williams & T. Johnston, 1658)

Gleeson, Janet, *The Arcanum* (New York: Warner Books, 1999)

Goldsmith, Oliver, *A History of the Earth and Animated Nature* (Glasgow: Blackie and Son, 1840)

Heikamp, Detlef, 'Seltene Nashörner in Martin Sperlich's Nashorngalerie und anderswo', in *Eine Festschrift für Martin Sperlich zu seinem sechzigsten Geburstag* (Tübingen, 1980), pp. 301–25

Loisel, Gustave, *Histoire des menageries de l'antiquité à nos jours* (Paris: Octave Doin et fils; Henri Laurens, 1912), 3 vols.

Machen, Arthur, ed., *The Memoirs of Jacques Casanova de Seingalt* (New York: Putnam, 1959–61).

Parsons, James, 'A letter from Dr Parsons to Martin Folkes, Esq.; President of the Royal Society, containing the natural history of the rhinoceros', *The Philosophical Transactions of the Royal Society*, vol. 42, no. 470, pp. 523–41

Quammen, David, *The Boilerplate Rhino: Nature in the Eye of the Beholder* (New York: Touchstone, 2001)

Radcliffe, Ann, *A Journey Made in the Summer of 1794, through Holland and the Western Frontier of Germany, with a return down the Rhine: to which are added, observations during a tour to the Lakes of Lancashire, Westmoreland and Cumberland* (Dublin: William Porter, 1795)

Louise E. Robbins, *Elephant Slaves and Pampered Parrots* (Johns Hopkins, 2002)

Roger, Jacques, *Buffon: un philosophe au jardin du roi* (Paris: Fayard, 1989)

Rookmaaker, Kees, and Jim Monson, 'Woodcuts and engravings illustrating the journey of Clara, the most popular Rhinoceros of the eighteenth century', *Der Zoologische Garten* N.F. 70:5 (Urban and Fischer, 2000), pp. 313–35

Rookmaaker, Leendert Cornelis, 'Captive rhinoceroses in Europe, from 1500 until 1810', *Bijdragen tot de Dierkunde*, vol. 43, no. 1, pp. 39–63

——, 'Two collections of rhinoceros plates compiled by James Douglas and James Parsons in the eighteenth century', *Journal of the Society for the Bibliography of Natural History*, vol. 9, no 1, pp. 17–38

——, 'Early rhinoceros systematics', in A. Wheeler and J. H. Price, eds., *History in the Service of Systematics* (London: Society for the Bibliography of Natural History Special Publication no. 1, 1981), pp. 111–18

——, *Bibliography of the Rhinoceros: An Analysis of the Literature on the Recent Rhinoceroses in Culture, History and Biology* (Rotterdam: A. A. Balkema, 1983)

Voltaire, *Le dictionnaire philosophique*, ed. Christine Mervaud (Paris: Universitas; Oxford: Voltaire Foundation, 1994)